LIVING LITURGY™

for Music Ministers

Year A • 2023

Verna Holyhead, SGS
Orin E. Johnson
Jessica Mannen Kimmet
Victoria McBride

LITURGICAL PRESS
Collegeville, Minnesota

www.litpress.org

Cover design by Monica Bokinskie. Art by Ruberval Monteiro da Silva, OSB.

ISSN 2573-0576

ISBN 978-0-8146-6726-2   978-0-8146-6727-9 (ebook)

Presented to

_____

in grateful appreciation
for your music ministry

_____

_____
(date)

USING THIS RESOURCE

Living Liturgy for Music Ministers™ is a resource intended to assist music ministers in their preparation for the liturgy on Sundays and selected solemnities, as well as Ash Wednesday. Included here are reflections on the gospel, and some insight into how the word of God informs daily life. It is hoped that the commentaries and reflections in this resource will assist music ministers with their own personal encounter with the sacred text. Music ministers who have a better understanding of the readings may be more apt to sing with a greater sensitivity to the deeper meaning of God's word.

Living Liturgy for Music Ministers™ has reflections on the gospel readings, brief commentaries connecting the gospel with the other readings, and reflections to assist psalmists with preparing for proclamation of the psalms. There are prayers provided for musicians to use with their own spiritual preparation for their ministry. Also included are the readings and responsorial psalms for every Sunday of the liturgical year, as well as for certain solemnities and Ash Wednesday. The second readings are found in an appendix.

This book is an essential resource for music ministers whose own spirituality is nourished by the liturgical cycle and the accompanying Scripture readings, especially the gospel and the psalm. The following outline suggests how this resource might be used by music ministers as they prepare for the liturgical assembly. Of course, adaptations are encouraged as there is no one "right" way to use this book.

On Monday, read only the gospel and reflect on it. Then, read "Reflecting on Living the Gospel" before reading the gospel again. What new insights come to mind? How does the reflection inform your understanding of the sacred text?

On Tuesday, read the first reading. What connections, if any, do you find between it and the gospel? This is a good time to read "Making Connections." What new insights come to mind for you? How do these readings inform the situation at your parish, or with your fellow music ministers?

On Wednesday, read the psalm in a prayerful manner. What connections do you draw between the psalm, the gospel, and the first reading? If it is helpful, read the second reading too and let the Scriptures percolate in your spiritual life, with insights bubbling up naturally. When we have been reading God's word, these insights happen not only in prayer but also throughout the week at home, at work, and in daily life.

On Thursday, spend some time with "Psalmist Preparation." How will you allow some of the spiritual insights you've gained through prayer to inform your proclamation of the psalm?

On Friday, if you haven't already been singing the psalm with your accompanist or fellow ministers, now is a good time to start—at least on your own, or *a cappella*. Use the "Prayer" together as a group or pray it on your own either before or after your practice.

On Saturday and Sunday, spend time in quiet prayer, allowing yourself to be an instrument in God's hands so that the gathered assembly might find meaning and spiritual insight through your ministry. In your prayer allow words or phrases from the gospel, psalm, and first and second readings to come to mind.

Many music ministers find this to be a rich ministry, filled with spirituality and giving new meaning to their daily lives. The personal encounter with the living and sacred text, being the vehicle through which the assembly hears God's word, and the fellowship one experiences throughout the week are sources of consolation and joy. When we minister with the gifts given to us by God, we become who we are meant to be. We actualize the charisms God has bestowed on us, not for our sakes alone, but for the building up of the Christian community. In this way, music ministers live their Christian baptism.

Gospel (Matt 24:37-44; L1A)

Jesus said to his disciples: "As it was in the days of Noah, so it will be at the coming of the Son of Man. In those days before the flood, they were eating and drinking, marrying and giving in marriage, up to the day that Noah entered the ark. They did not know until the flood came and carried them all away. So will it be also at the coming of the Son of Man. Two men will be out in the field; one will be taken, and one will be left. Two women will be grinding at the mill; one will be taken, and one will be left. Therefore, stay awake! For you do not know on which day your Lord will come. Be sure of this: if the master of the house had known the hour of night when the thief was coming, he would have stayed awake and not let his house be broken into. So too, you also must be prepared, for at an hour you do not expect, the Son of Man will come."

First Reading (Isa 2:1-5)

This is what Isaiah, son of Amoz,
    saw concerning Judah and Jerusalem.
      In days to come,
    the mountain of the Lord's house
      shall be established as the highest mountain
      and raised above the hills.
All nations shall stream toward it;
      many peoples shall come and say:
"Come, let us climb the Lord's mountain,
      to the house of the God of Jacob,
that he may instruct us in his ways,
      and we may walk in his paths."
For from Zion shall go forth instruction,
      and the word of the Lord from Jerusalem.
He shall judge between the nations,
      and impose terms on many peoples.
They shall beat their swords into plowshares
      and their spears into pruning hooks;

one nation shall not raise the sword against another,
nor shall they train for war again.
O house of Jacob, come,
let us walk in the light of the Lᴏʀᴅ!

Responsorial Psalm (Ps 122:1-2, 3-4, 4-5, 6-7, 8-9)

℞. Let us go rejoicing to the house of the Lord.

I rejoiced because they said to me,
"We will go up to the house of the Lᴏʀᴅ."
And now we have set foot
within your gates, O Jerusalem.

℞. Let us go rejoicing to the house of the Lord.

Jerusalem, built as a city
with compact unity.
To it the tribes go up,
the tribes of the Lᴏʀᴅ.

℞. Let us go rejoicing to the house of the Lord.

According to the decree for Israel,
to give thanks to the name of the Lᴏʀᴅ.
In it are set up judgment seats,
seats for the house of David.

℞. Let us go rejoicing to the house of the Lord.

Pray for the peace of Jerusalem!
May those who love you prosper!
May peace be within your walls,
prosperity in your buildings.

℞. Let us go rejoicing to the house of the Lord.

Because of my brothers and friends
I will say, "Peace be within you!"
Because of the house of the Lᴏʀᴅ, our God,
I will pray for your good.

℞. Let us go rejoicing to the house of the Lord.

See Appendix, p. 210, for Second Reading

Reflecting on Living the Gospel

At the beginning of the liturgical year, the church tries to make us more attentive to, hopeful about, and prepared for the moment of the great advent of God. For the whole of creation, it will be the *eschaton*, the "end time" not so much *of* the world but *for* the world. Individually and cosmically, this will be a new birth, as unimaginable and yet so much more hugely real than the world that awaited us when we were born from our mother's womb.

Making Connections

Compared to the gospel, the first reading offers a more comforting and joyful vision of the end times. There is unity and inclusion rather than division; all are called to be part of the lasting peace God envisions for us. The psalmist echoes the joy of the nations streaming toward Jerusalem as he, too, heads there on pilgrimage and prays for its peace. The second reading gives us practical ways to "stay awake," through moral conduct and union with Christ.

Psalmist Preparation

This is a pilgrimage song, one that invites participation in the festal journey to Jerusalem. This trip was an obligation but is here received as a joy. Does your attendance and ministry at liturgy feel more like an obligation or a joy to you? What might be keeping you from the sort of joy the psalmist expresses here? As you prepare this psalm, pray for all who will attend Mass this week only out of obligation. Thank God for their presence; sometimes, going through the motions is a way of witnessing to love as a virtue when feelings of joy are escaping us.

Prayer

God of Heaven and Earth,
you long to be our God; we long to draw near to you.
Show unto us the path to your holy city,
that all may cry out with joy:
"Let us go rejoicing to the house of the Lord."
Through Christ our Lord.
Amen.

Gospel (Matt 3:1-12; L4A)

John the Baptist appeared, preaching in the desert of Judea and saying, "Repent, for the kingdom of heaven is at hand!" It was of him that the prophet Isaiah had spoken when he said:

> A voice of one crying out in
>   the desert,
> Prepare the way of the Lord,
>   make straight his paths.

John wore clothing made of camel's hair and had a leather belt around his waist. His food was locusts and wild honey. At that time Jerusalem, all Judea, and the whole region around the Jordan were going out to him and were being baptized by him in the Jordan River as they acknowledged their sins.

When he saw many of the Pharisees and Sadducees coming to his baptism, he said to them, "You brood of vipers! Who warned you to flee from the coming wrath? Produce good fruit as evidence of your repentance. And do not presume to say to yourselves, 'We have Abraham as our father.' For I tell you, God can raise up children to Abraham from these stones. Even now the ax lies at the root of the trees. Therefore every tree that does not bear good fruit will be cut down and thrown into the fire. I am baptizing you with water, for repentance, but the one who is coming after me is mightier than I. I am not worthy to carry his sandals. He will baptize you with the Holy Spirit and fire. His winnowing fan is in his hand. He will clear his threshing floor and gather his wheat into his barn, but the chaff he will burn with unquenchable fire."

First Reading (Isa 11:1-10)

On that day, a shoot shall sprout from the stump of Jesse,
  and from his roots a bud shall blossom.
The spirit of the LORD shall rest upon him:
  a spirit of wisdom and of understanding,
a spirit of counsel and of strength,
  a spirit of knowledge and of fear of the Lord,
  and his delight shall be the fear of the LORD.
Not by appearance shall he judge,
  nor by hearsay shall he decide,

but he shall judge the poor with justice,
    and decide aright for the land's afflicted.
He shall strike the ruthless with the rod of his mouth,
    and with the breath of his lips he shall slay the wicked.
Justice shall be the band around his waist,
    and faithfulness a belt upon his hips.
Then the wolf shall be a guest of the lamb,
    and the leopard shall lie down with the kid;
the calf and the young lion shall browse together,
    with a little child to guide them.
The cow and the bear shall be neighbors,
    together their young shall rest;
    the lion shall eat hay like the ox.
The baby shall play by the cobra's den,
    and the child lay his hand on the adder's lair.
There shall be no harm or ruin on all my holy mountain;
    for the earth shall be filled with knowledge of the LORD,
    as water covers the sea.
On that day, the root of Jesse,
    set up as a signal for the nations,
the Gentiles shall seek out,
    for his dwelling shall be glorious.

Responsorial Psalm (Ps 72:1-2, 7-8, 12-13, 17)

℞. (cf. 7) Justice shall flourish in his time, and fullness of peace for ever.

O God, with your judgment endow the king,
    and with your justice, the king's son;
he shall govern your people with justice
    and your afflicted ones with judgment.

℞. Justice shall flourish in his time, and fullness of peace for ever.

Justice shall flower in his days,
    and profound peace, till the moon be no more.
May he rule from sea to sea,
    and from the River to the ends of the earth.

℞. Justice shall flourish in his time, and fullness of peace for ever.

For he shall rescue the poor when he cries out,
  and the afflicted when he has no one to help him.
He shall have pity for the lowly and the poor;
  the lives of the poor he shall save.

R̸. Justice shall flourish in his time, and fullness of peace for ever.

May his name be blessed forever;
  as long as the sun his name shall remain.
In him shall all the tribes of the earth be blessed;
  all the nations shall proclaim his happiness.

R̸. Justice shall flourish in his time, and fullness of peace for ever.

See Appendix, p. 210, for Second Reading

Reflecting on Living the Gospel

Sunday after Sunday during the four weeks of Advent, we light a candle on the Advent wreath: a fragile flame that reminds us that in these weeks we are preparing to renew the welcome into our lives of the vulnerable One who was announced by a star rising in the darkness and a song echoing through the night. Jesus still comes when we seem to be starved of stars and can find little to sing about. Then, in faith, we can rejoice.

Making Connections

Again, a harsh-sounding gospel is paired with an Old Testament prophecy of lush comfort. At the same time, though, it echoes the gospel's promise that Jesus is not coming to bring peace alone; those who are unrepentantly wicked or ruthless should be afraid of his coming. The second reading affirms that Christ's coming is for all; it is not our background or origin that matters but our choice to follow Jesus.

Psalmist Preparation

We often associate the word "justice" with criminal justice, with those who do wrong being made to pay some kind of retribution for their offenses. Justice involves people getting what they deserve. In this psalm, though, we see that the heart of justice is indeed about people getting their due, but what they are owed not as wrongdoers but as beloved children of God. The justice with which this King is concerned is justice that protects the poor, recognizing the dignity of all who seem lowly by our worldly standards. This is a justice that brings "profound peace." Rest in the alliteration and imagery of that phrase; there's a powerful depth to it. Try praying with this line this week, inviting your own heart into the profundity of the peace God promises.

Prayer

God of the Lowly and Poor,
we await the coming of your son, Jesus,
who shall make everything whole.
Justice shall flourish in his time, and fullness of peace forever.
May he come to us quickly, without delay,
he who is compassion and mercy.
Amen.

Gospel (Luke 1:26-38; L689)

The angel Gabriel was sent from God to a town of Galilee called Nazareth, to a virgin betrothed to a man named Joseph, of the house of David, and the virgin's name was Mary. And coming to her, he said, "Hail, full of grace! The Lord is with you." But she was greatly troubled at what was said and pondered what sort of greeting this might be. Then the angel said to her, "Do not be afraid, Mary, for you have found favor with God. Behold, you will conceive in your womb and bear a son, and you shall name him Jesus. He will be great and will be called Son of the Most
High, and the Lord God will give him the throne of David his father, and he will rule over the house of Jacob forever, and of his Kingdom there will be no end." But Mary said to the angel, "How can this be, since I have no relations with a man?" And the angel said to her in reply, "The Holy Spirit will come upon you, and the power of the Most High will overshadow you. Therefore the child to be born will be called holy, the Son of God. And behold, Elizabeth, your relative, has also conceived a son in her old age, and this is the sixth month for her who was called barren; for nothing will be impossible for God." Mary said, "Behold, I am the handmaid of the Lord. May it be done to me according to your word." Then the angel departed from her.

First Reading (Gen 3:9-15, 20)

After the man, Adam, had eaten of the tree, the LORD God called to the man and asked him, "Where are you?" He answered, "I heard you in the garden; but I was afraid, because I was naked, so I hid myself." Then he asked, "Who told you that you were naked? You have eaten, then, from the tree of which I had forbidden you to eat!" The man replied, "The woman whom you put here with me— she gave me fruit from the tree, and so I ate it." The LORD God then asked the woman, "Why did you do such a thing?" The woman answered, "The serpent tricked me into it, so I ate it."

Then the Lord God said to the serpent:

"Because you have done this, you shall be banned
  from all the animals
  and from all the wild creatures;
on your belly shall you crawl,
  and dirt shall you eat
  all the days of your life.
I will put enmity between you and the woman,
  and between your offspring and hers;
he will strike at your head,
  while you strike at his heel."

The man called his wife Eve, because she became the mother of all the living.

Responsorial Psalm (Ps 98:1, 2-3ab, 3cd-4)

℟. (1a) Sing to the Lord a new song, for he has done marvelous deeds.

Sing to the Lord a new song,
  for he has done wondrous deeds;
his right hand has won victory for him,
  his holy arm.

℟. Sing to the Lord a new song, for he has done marvelous deeds.

The Lord has made his salvation known:
  in the sight of the nations he has revealed his justice.
He has remembered his kindness and his faithfulness
  toward the house of Israel.

℟. Sing to the Lord a new song, for he has done marvelous deeds.

All the ends of the earth have seen
  the salvation by our God.
Sing joyfully to the Lord, all you lands;
  break into song; sing praise.

℟. Sing to the Lord a new song, for he has done marvelous deeds.

See Appendix, p. 210, for Second Reading

Reflecting on Living the Gospel

As we navigate the deep waters and crossroads we encounter in our lives, we can look upon them with the eyes of Mary. We can look for signs and symbols that indicate that God is speaking to us and attempting to stay close to us. We can look to those who have come before us for the wisdom and witness they have to offer. When we notice these things, we can trust that the voice we hear is indeed the voice of God, and like Mary, we can respond with a trust-filled "yes."

Making Connections

Like Mary, our response to God's invitation requires courage, generosity of spirit, and a willingness to live for others. May today's celebration inspire us to respond similarly, making the words, "Do not be afraid," our own.

Psalmist Preparation

Today's readings don't give us the *Magnificat*, that great song of joy and triumph that Mary sings after the Visitation. But this psalm, which Mary would have known and prayed with, foreshadows its themes. God's power and victory and righteousness are affirmed and proclaimed. So is God's memory, as God remembers and fulfills God's promises. This is a sign of tender love and care; we all long to be remembered and feel special when we are. God is both powerful enough to change the course of world history and personal enough to hold each of us as a beloved individual. As you prepare this psalm, re-read the *Magnificat* (Luke 1:46-55). Note its similarities to this psalm and envision yourself singing its lavish praise alongside Mary. Generous gratitude is our response to God's generous goodness.

Prayer

Victorious God of All Peoples,
We rejoice in your salvation, your kindness, your faithfulness.
Inspire in us *a new song,* for you have *done marvelous deeds.*
Grant us a desire and dedication to share your good news
with the whole world, waiting, and in need.
Amen.

Gospel (Matt 11:2-11; L7A)

When John the Baptist heard in prison of the works of the Christ, he sent his disciples to Jesus with this question, "Are you the one who is to come, or should we look for another?" Jesus said to them in reply, "Go and tell John what you hear and see: the blind regain their sight, the lame walk, lepers are cleansed, the deaf hear, the dead are raised, and the poor have the good news proclaimed to them. And blessed is the one who takes no offense at me."

As they were going off, Jesus began to speak to the crowds about John, "What did you go out to the desert to see? A reed swayed by the wind? Then what did you go out to see? Someone dressed in fine clothing? Those who wear fine clothing are in royal palaces. Then why did you go out? To see a prophet? Yes, I tell you, and more than a prophet. This is the one about whom it is written:

> *Behold, I am sending my messenger ahead of you;*
> *he will prepare your way before you.*

Amen, I say to you, among those born of women there has been none greater than John the Baptist; yet the least in the kingdom of heaven is greater than he."

First Reading (Isa 35:1-6a, 10)

The desert and the parched land will exult;
    the steppe will rejoice and bloom.
They will bloom with abundant flowers,
    and rejoice with joyful song.
The glory of Lebanon will be given to them,
    the splendor of Carmel and Sharon;
they will see the glory of the LORD,
    the splendor of our God.
Strengthen the hands that are feeble,
    make firm the knees that are weak,
say to those whose hearts are frightened:
    Be strong, fear not!

Here is your God,
>he comes with vindication;
with divine recompense
>he comes to save you.
Then will the eyes of the blind be opened,
>the ears of the deaf be cleared;
then will the lame leap like a stag,
>then the tongue of the mute will sing.

Those whom the LORD has ransomed will return
>and enter Zion singing,
>crowned with everlasting joy;
they will meet with joy and gladness,
>sorrow and mourning will flee.

Responsorial Psalm (Ps 146:6-7, 8-9, 9-10)

R̸. (cf. Isaiah 35:4) Lord, come and save us. *or:* R̸. Alleluia.

The LORD God keeps faith forever,
>secures justice for the oppressed,
>gives food to the hungry.
The LORD sets captives free.

R̸. Lord, come and save us. *or:* R̸. Alleluia.

The LORD gives sight to the blind;
>the LORD raises up those who were bowed down.
The LORD loves the just;
>the LORD protects strangers.

R̸. Lord, come and save us. *or:* R̸. Alleluia.

The fatherless and the widow he sustains,
>but the way of the wicked he thwarts.
The LORD shall reign forever;
>your God, O Zion, through all generations.

R̸. Lord, come and save us. *or:* R̸. Alleluia.

See Appendix, p. 210, for Second Reading

Reflecting on Living the Gospel

John the Baptist ended up in Herod's prison, and there he would lose his head, but never his heart, to that king's lack of integrity and fear of losing face. John's heart had been lost long ago to Jesus, and no doubt the message sent back to him in prison confirmed John in his love and offered him the truth that the way to deep faith so often goes through deep doubt. Do we, at least to some degree, measure up to such praise—or blame?

Making Connections

The future tense of the first reading transforms into present tense in the gospel. With Jesus's coming, the blind *do* see, the deaf *do* hear, here and now. Jesus's presence is effecting healing and change as his earthly ministry begins. It is still effecting healing now as his presence continues with us in countless harder-to-see ways. And yet Advent is also our season of waiting; the second reading reminds us that we are still waiting for Christ's healing work to be accomplished in its fullness. The transformation of our world has yet to be complete.

Psalmist Preparation

The psalm contains all the dramatic tension of Advent: God's verbs are all in present tense, affirming who God is and what God does. And yet the response still cries out to God, pleading that God come and save us. God is here already; the fullest realization of God's promises is yet to be seen. As you prepare this psalm, think of one way you have witnessed God's work in your life, as well as one area where you still need Christ's coming. Keep these in mind as you proclaim this psalm to a congregation full of people with stories just like yours, full of both joys and sorrows, abundance and lack.

Prayer

Voice of the Oppressed,
you are divine power for those in need,
the oppressed, the hungry, the captive.
Bring your healing, bring your justice;
come to reign over us forever.
Lord, come and save us,
we who patiently await your coming.
Amen.

Gospel (Luke 1:26-38; L690A [or Luke 1:39-47])

The angel Gabriel was sent from God to a town of Galilee called Nazareth, to a virgin betrothed to a man named Joseph, of the house of David, and the virgin's name was Mary. And coming to her, he said, "Hail, full of grace! The Lord is with you." But she was greatly troubled at what was said and pondered what sort of greeting this might be. Then the angel said to her, "Do not be afraid, Mary, for you have found favor with God. Behold, you will conceive in your womb and bear a son, and you shall name him Jesus. He will be great and will be called Son of the

Most High, and the Lord God will give him the throne of David his father, and he will rule over the house of Jacob forever, and of his Kingdom there will be no end." But Mary said to the angel, "How can this be, since I have no relations with a man?" And the angel said to her in reply, "The Holy Spirit will come upon you, and the power of the Most High will overshadow you. Therefore the child to be born will be called holy, the Son of God. And behold, Elizabeth, your relative, has also conceived a son in her old age, and this is the sixth month for her who was called barren; for nothing will be impossible for God." Mary said, "Behold, I am the handmaid of the Lord. May it be done to me according to your word." Then the angel departed from her.

First Reading (Rev 11:19a; 12:1-6a, 10ab [or Zech 2:14-17])

God's temple in heaven was opened, and the ark of his covenant could be seen in the temple.

A great sign appeared in the sky, a woman clothed with the sun, with the moon under her feet, and on her head a crown of twelve stars. She was with child and wailed aloud in pain as she labored to give birth. Then another sign appeared in the sky; it was a huge red dragon, with seven heads and ten horns, and on its heads were seven diadems. Its tail swept away a third of the stars in the sky and hurled them down to the earth. Then the dragon stood before the woman about to give birth, to devour her child when she gave birth. She gave birth to a son, a male child, destined to rule all the nations with an iron rod. Her child was caught up to God and his throne. The woman herself fled into the desert where she had a place prepared by God.

Then I heard a loud voice in heaven say: "Now have salvation and power come, and the Kingdom of our God and the authority of his Anointed."

Responsorial Psalm (Jdt 13:18bcde, 19)

R̸. (15:9d) You are the highest honor of our race.

Blessed are you, daughter, by the Most High God,
above all the women on earth;
and blessed be the LORD God,
the creator of heaven and earth.

R̸. You are the highest honor of our race.

Your deed of hope will never be forgotten
by those who tell of the might of God.

R̸. You are the highest honor of our race.

Reflecting on Living the Gospel

Juan Diego believed in the truth of his encounter with the Blessed Virgin and because of his faith, the indigenous community in sixteenth-century Mexico received a sign that God cares about their needs and will always bend a compassionate ear toward their concerns. The story of Juan Diego and Our Lady of Guadalupe is a reminder that God continues to seek us out. In every land and in every time period, God will choose the lowly ones for partnership and will bestow upon all people comfort and care.

Making Connections

As we celebrate the patron of the Americas in today's feast, may we be mindful of the many ways God reveals "God-self" to us. God is not limited or confined to our own understanding or imagination. Rather, God transcends the self-constructed barriers and limitations we sometimes uphold and even idolize.

Psalmist Preparation

Strictly speaking, today you sing not a psalm but an Old Testament canticle, another kind of sung prayer. This canticle appears in the book of Judith, when a woman of faith and courage becomes a force in her own right, one who delivers Israel from certain defeat. If you don't know the story of Judith, take some time to read it so that you are familiar with this canticle's context. At this Marian feast, we reassign these words to Mary. Her story is different from Judith's in many ways, but in both, God invites someone unexpected to take on a unique role in saving God's people. Both women—one a virgin who gives birth, one a widow who deals death—are remembered for their "deed of hope." Both women, through their faith and courage, become indispensable parts of God's story of salvation.

Prayer

God of Power and Might,
you choose the lowly among us to bring to birth
your words of justice and peace.
You chose Mary, the *highest honor of our race*, to bring to birth
your Word: Jesus, justice and peace incarnate.
May we also embody such holiness in all we say and do.
Amen.

Gospel (Matt 1:18-24; L10A)

This is how the birth of Jesus Christ came about. When his mother Mary was betrothed to Joseph, but before they lived together, she was found with child through the Holy Spirit. Joseph her husband, since he was a righteous man, yet unwilling to expose her to shame, decided to divorce her quietly. Such was his intention when, behold, the angel of the Lord appeared to him in a dream and said, "Joseph, son of David, do not be afraid to take Mary your wife into your home. For it is through the Holy Spirit

that this child has been conceived in her. She will bear a son and you are to name him Jesus, because he will save his people from their sins." All this took place to fulfill what the Lord had said through the prophet:

> *Behold, the virgin shall conceive and bear a son,*
> *and they shall name him Emmanuel,*

which means "God is with us." When Joseph awoke, he did as the angel of the Lord had commanded him and took his wife into his home.

First Reading (Isa 7:10-14)

The LORD spoke to Ahaz, saying: Ask for a sign from the LORD, your God; let it be deep as the netherworld, or high as the sky! But Ahaz answered, "I will not ask! I will not tempt the LORD!" Then Isaiah said: Listen, O house of David! Is it not enough for you to weary people, must you also weary my God? Therefore the Lord himself will give you this sign: the virgin shall conceive, and bear a son, and shall name him Emmanuel.

Responsorial Psalm (Ps 24:1-2, 3-4, 5-6)

℟. (7c and 10b) Let the Lord enter; he is king of glory.

The LORD's are the earth and its fullness;
>   the world and those who dwell in it.
For he founded it upon the seas
>   and established it upon the rivers.

℟. Let the Lord enter; he is king of glory.

Who can ascend the mountain of the LORD?
   or who may stand in his holy place?
One whose hands are sinless, whose heart is clean,
   who desires not what is vain.

R℣. Let the Lord enter; he is king of glory.

He shall receive a blessing from the LORD,
   a reward from God his savior.
Such is the race that seeks for him,
   that seeks the face of the God of Jacob.

R℣. Let the Lord enter; he is king of glory.

See Appendix, p. 211, for Second Reading

Reflecting on Living the Gospel

Joseph is cast by Matthew along the lines of another Joseph, the patriarch of Genesis, also a man of dreams (Gen 37; 40) and of God's providence (Gen 45:1-15). Out of the granaries of Egypt over which he was the Pharaoh's chief steward, Joseph cared for his family in time of famine. The Joseph of the gospel also cares unobtrusively for his family, stewarding the Grain and the Bread that continues to feed our hunger at every eucharistic assembly.

Making Connections

Isaiah's prophecy is so extraordinary that it is not recognized as a sign when it finally occurs in Mary; the presumption is that this virgin's conception is not God's work but a very ordinary moment of human sin and weakness. Our Advent theme continues: this is a God who defies expectations and comes in ways for which we are not ready. In the second reading, Paul packs a lot of theology into the opening of his letter, echoing the idea of Christ's dual origin: fully human, fully divine.

Psalmist Preparation

In our final week of preparation for Christmas, we call on the Lord to finally enter—to enter our world, our history, our hearts. As you prepare this psalm, think of one specific way you hope the Lord will enter your life in the coming season. Hold that intention close as you proclaim the earnest plea of the psalm. Pray also that you and all gathered this week will have your eyes opened to all the ways that God has already entered and is continually entering lives, often in unseen or unrecognized ways.

Prayer

God on High, God with Us,
You once visited your people in need of a savior;
today your people still seek your face.
We cry, *Let the Lord enter; he is king of glory,*
and with longing await you who are salvation and restoration.
May that time come soon, maranatha!
Amen.

DECEMBER 25, 2022

Gospel **(Matt 1:1-25 [or Matt 1:18-25]; L13 ABC)**

The book of the genealogy of Jesus Christ, the son of David, the son of Abraham.

Abraham became the father of Isaac, Isaac the father of Jacob, Jacob the father of Judah and his brothers. Judah became the father of Perez and Zerah, whose mother was Tamar. Perez became the father of Hezron, Hezron the father of Ram, Ram the father of Amminadab. Amminadab became the father of Nahshon, Nahshon the father of Salmon, Salmon the father of Boaz, whose mother was Rahab. Boaz became the father of Obed, whose mother was Ruth. Obed became the father of Jesse, Jesse the father of David the king.

David became the father of Solomon, whose mother had been the wife of Uriah. Solomon became the father of Rehoboam, Rehoboam the father of Abijah, Abijah the father of Asaph. Asaph became the father of Jehoshaphat, Jehoshaphat the father of Joram, Joram the father of Uzziah. Uzziah became the father of Jotham, Jotham the father of Ahaz, Ahaz the father of Hezekiah. Hezekiah became the father of Manasseh, Manasseh the father of Amos, Amos the father of Josiah. Josiah became the father of Jechoniah and his brothers at the time of the Babylonian exile.

After the Babylonian exile, Jechoniah became the father of Shealtiel, Shealtiel the father of Zerubbabel, Zerubbabel the father of Abiud. Abiud became the father of Eliakim, Eliakim the father of Azor, Azor the father of Zadok. Zadok became the father of Achim, Achim the father of Eliud, Eliud the father of Eleazar. Eleazar became the father of Matthan, Matthan the father of Jacob, Jacob the father of Joseph, the husband of Mary. Of her was born Jesus who is called the Christ.

Thus the total number of generations from Abraham to David is fourteen generations; from David to the Babylonian exile, fourteen generations; from the Babylonian exile to the Christ, fourteen generations.

Now this is how the birth of Jesus Christ came about. When his mother Mary was betrothed to Joseph, but before they lived together, she was found with child through the Holy Spirit. Joseph her husband, since he was a righteous man, yet unwilling to expose her to shame, decided to divorce her quietly. Such was his intention when, behold, the angel of the Lord appeared to him in a dream and said, "Joseph, son of David, do not be afraid to take Mary your wife into your home. For it is through the Holy Spirit that this child has been conceived in her. She will bear a son and you are to name him Jesus, because he will save his people from their sins." All this took place to fulfill what the Lord had said through the prophet:

> Behold, the virgin shall conceive and bear a son,
>   and they shall name him Emmanuel,

which means "God is with us." When Joseph awoke, he did as the angel of the Lord had commanded him and took his wife into his home. He had no relations with her until she bore a son, and he named him Jesus.

First Reading (Isa 62:1-5)

For Zion's sake I will not be silent,
    for Jerusalem's sake I will not be quiet,
until her vindication shines forth like the dawn
    and her victory like a burning torch.

Nations shall behold your vindication,
    and all the kings your glory;
you shall be called by a new name
    pronounced by the mouth of the LORD.
You shall be a glorious crown in the hand of the LORD,
    a royal diadem held by your God.
No more shall people call you "Forsaken,"
    or your land "Desolate,"
but you shall be called "My Delight,"
    and your land "Espoused."
For the LORD delights in you
    and makes your land his spouse.
As a young man marries a virgin,
    your Builder shall marry you;
and as a bridegroom rejoices in his bride
    so shall your God rejoice in you.

Responsorial Psalm (Ps 89:4-5, 16-17, 27, 29)

R̸. (2a) For ever I will sing the goodness of the Lord.

I have made a covenant with my chosen one,
    I have sworn to David my servant:
forever will I confirm your posterity
    and establish your throne for all generations.

R̸. For ever I will sing the goodness of the Lord.

Blessed the people who know the joyful shout;
    in the light of your countenance, O LORD, they walk.
At your name they rejoice all the day,
    and through your justice they are exalted.

℟. For ever I will sing the goodness of the Lord.

He shall say of me, "You are my father,
    my God, the Rock, my savior."
Forever I will maintain my kindness toward him,
    and my covenant with him stands firm.

℟. For ever I will sing the goodness of the Lord.

See Appendix, p. 211, for Second Reading

Reflecting on Living the Gospel

Matthew provides a genealogy that traces the lineage of Jesus Christ. Regardless of their deeds or accolades, their foibles and failures, everyone included is significant because they are the stepping-stones that led us to Jesus Christ.

In his 2017 address at the Ignatian Teach-In for Social Justice, Fr. Bryan Massingale used the image of a relay race to describe how every person plays a part in bringing about the kingdom of God. The work is not ours to finish, but it is our duty to do our part. To remain faithful to this charge, it can be helpful to look back on the stories of those who came before us.

Making Connections

It might be tempting to skip today's gospel from Matthew in favor of the familiar Lukan account of Jesus's birth. After all, can anyone actually pronounce all those names in the genealogy of Jesus? God's promise of salvation permeates today's readings and the entire reality of the Incarnation. God is faithful to God's people, from Abraham and Sarah, to Joseph and Mary, to all people today.

Psalmist Preparation

Promising to sing forever is a big promise! But most of the "forevers" in this psalm refer to God's action, not ours, and we do our best to respond to God's ongoing goodness with ongoing gratitude. As you prepare to proclaim this psalm, reflect on where you are this Christmas. Is your faith in a place that feels good? Do you feel the joy of Christmas? Do you *want* to sing God's praises right now? Or are you perhaps in a less fruitful season, one of waiting or frustration with God or spiritual dryness? Either way, God is with you. Either way, you can choose to sing of God's goodness and even lead others to it. Either way, your song is legitimate, and it is heard and beloved by God.

Prayer

God of Isaiah, Jesse, David, and Mary,
you draw near to us today, in kindness and in truth.
Generations have awaited you;
in this moment let each heart cry out:
Forever I will sing the goodness of the Lord.
You are Emmanuel, "God is With Us."
Remain with us, now and always.
Amen.

DECEMBER 25, 2022

Gospel (Luke 2:1-14; L14ABC)

In those days a decree went out from Caesar Augustus that the whole world should be enrolled. This was the first enrollment, when Quirinius was governor of Syria. So all went to be enrolled, each to his own town. And Joseph too went up from Galilee from the town of Nazareth to Judea, to the city of David that is called Bethlehem, because he was of the house and family of David, to be enrolled with Mary, his betrothed, who was with child. While they were there, the time came for her to have her child, and she gave birth to her firstborn son. She wrapped him in swaddling clothes and laid him in a manger, because there was no room for them in the inn.

Now there were shepherds in that region living in the fields and keeping the night watch over their flock. The angel of the Lord appeared to them and the glory of the Lord shone around them, and they were struck with great fear. The angel said to them, "Do not be afraid; for behold, I proclaim to you good news of great joy that will be for all the people. For today in the city of David a savior has been born for you who is Christ and Lord. And this will be a sign for you: you will find an infant wrapped in swaddling clothes and lying in a manger." And suddenly there was a multitude of the heavenly host with the angel, praising God and saying:

> "Glory to God in the highest
>   and on earth peace to those on whom his favor rests."

First Reading (Isa 9:1-6)

> The people who walked in darkness
>   have seen a great light;
> upon those who dwelt in the land of gloom
>   a light has shone.
> You have brought them abundant joy
>   and great rejoicing,
> as they rejoice before you as at the harvest,
>   as people make merry when dividing spoils.
> For the yoke that burdened them,
>   the pole on their shoulder,
> and the rod of their taskmaster
>   you have smashed, as on the day of Midian.

For every boot that tramped in battle,
   every cloak rolled in blood,
   will be burned as fuel for flames.
For a child is born to us, a son is given us;
   upon his shoulder dominion rests.
They name him Wonder-Counselor, God-Hero,
   Father-Forever, Prince of Peace.
His dominion is vast
   and forever peaceful,
from David's throne, and over his kingdom,
   which he confirms and sustains
by judgment and justice,
   both now and forever.
The zeal of the LORD of hosts will do this!

Responsorial Psalm (Ps 96:1-2, 2-3, 11-12, 13)

R7. (Luke 2:11) Today is born our Savior, Christ the Lord.

Sing to the LORD a new song;
   sing to the LORD, all you lands.
Sing to the LORD; bless his name.

R7. Today is born our Savior, Christ the Lord.

Announce his salvation, day after day.
   Tell his glory among the nations;
   among all peoples, his wondrous deeds.

R7. Today is born our Savior, Christ the Lord.

Let the heavens be glad and the earth rejoice;
   let the sea and what fills it resound;
   let the plains be joyful and all that is in them!
Then shall all the trees of the forest exult.

R7. Today is born our Savior, Christ the Lord.

They shall exult before the LORD, for he comes;
   for he comes to rule the earth.
He shall rule the world with justice
   and the peoples with his constancy.

R7. Today is born our Savior, Christ the Lord.

See Appendix, p. 211, for Second Reading

Reflecting on Living the Gospel

On this night, we hear the story of Christ's birth. The timing of Jesus's arrival was neither ideal nor negotiable. There was not even time to secure adequate accommodations and Jesus Christ, the Son of God, was born in a stable and laid in a manger. Through this, we are reminded that God is prepared to do miraculous things in the midst of our everyday lives whether or not we are prepared for them. In other words, God's time will always have the final say. Sometimes, we need to be jolted out of those routines so that we can remember the sacredness and divine potential of each moment.

Making Connections

Almost all Christmas scenes include the shepherds named in today's gospel. In fact, it is hard to even imagine a nativity scene without the shepherds. "Of course they were there," we say. We must remember, however, that God's revelation to the shepherds in the field was nothing short of extraordinary. During Jesus's time, shepherds were a nomadic people, often without any status or power. Even so, these were the first to hear the news of the birth of Christ. How might we continue to uphold the voices and experiences of all people, regardless of status or power?

Psalmist Preparation

In this psalm, we claim that seas and plains and trees and animals all join in our great song of praise for what God has done for us. God's entry into human life changes the course of history—not just for humanity but for all of God's creatures. All our relationships, including our broken relationship with the earth, are being healed by God's presence. As part of your preparation to proclaim this psalm, reflect on how God's creation participates in the praise of God. How is creation proclaiming God's goodness to you in your particular part of the world?

Prayer

Ever-Constant God,
you who always offer your people love, mercy, and salvation,
we give thanks for the gift of your son, the fullness of your self-giving.
Today is born our savior, Christ the Lord.
Born to set us free, let all creation exult and be glad!
Glory to God!
Amen.

Gospel (Luke 2:15-20; L15ABC)

When the angels went away from them to heaven, the shepherds said to one another, "Let us go, then, to Bethlehem to see this thing that has taken place, which the Lord has made known to us." So they went in haste and found Mary and Joseph, and the infant lying in the manger. When they saw this, they made known the message that had been told them about this child. All who heard it were amazed by what had been told them by the shepherds. And Mary kept all these things, reflecting on them in her heart. Then the shepherds returned, glorifying and praising God for all they had heard and seen, just as it had been told to them.

First Reading (Isa 62:11-12)

See, the LORD proclaims
    to the ends of the earth:
say to daughter Zion,
    your savior comes!
Here is his reward with him,
    his recompense before him.
They shall be called the holy people,
    the redeemed of the LORD,
and you shall be called "Frequented,"
    a city that is not forsaken.

Responsorial Psalm (Ps 97:1, 6, 11-12)

R℣. A light will shine on us this day: the Lord is born for us.

The LORD is king; let the earth rejoice;
    let the many isles be glad.
The heavens proclaim his justice,
    and all peoples see his glory.

R℣. A light will shine on us this day: the Lord is born for us.

Light dawns for the just;
and gladness, for the upright of heart.
Be glad in the Lᴏʀᴅ, you just,
and give thanks to his holy name.
℞. A light will shine on us this day: the Lord is born for us.

See Appendix, p. 211, for Second Reading

Reflecting on Living the Gospel

As we celebrate the birth of our Lord Jesus Christ, how can we seek Jesus more intentionally? Where in our lives can we look to see hope being born anew? If we follow the example of the shepherds and seek out Jesus, who knows what miracles we will discover? As we celebrate this Christmas season, we would do well to sit and ponder the mysteries that God presents to us. This too is a way of proclaiming the good news. When God's words permeate our hearts we will be able to see the world with new eyes.

Making Connections

In his book, *Light of the World,* Hans Urs von Balthasar writes, "Christmas is not an event within history but is rather the invasion of time by eternity." God's self-gift in the Incarnation fundamentally and forever changes our reality. Do we recognize God present in all people? Do we treat others with dignity and respect, knowing that through the Incarnation, God is intimately present within them? May we, like the shepherds in today's gospel, be so moved by God's self-gift that we glorify and praise God for all that we have seen and heard.

Psalmist Preparation

At this dawn Mass, you get to sing about light. This is an apt image for the coming of Christ, whose light breaks through the darkness of sin and death and illumines our way to the freedom and peace that only God can give. Even the more secular side of Christmas celebration embraces the use of light, covering our homes and shopping centers and Christmas trees with twinkly bits of brightness. As you prepare this psalm, spend some time noticing and reflecting on the lights you see at this time of year. Let them be a reminder of Christ's coming.

Prayer

God of Generous Love,
you are a beacon always in the shadows and darkness,
guiding us on our journey of holiness.
A light will shine on us this day: the Lord is born for us.
Let us hasten to seek you in our midst,
and glorify and praise your holy name.
Amen.

DECEMBER 25, 2022

Gospel (John 1:1-18 [or John 1:1-5, 9-14]; L16ABC)

In the beginning was the Word,
  and the Word was with God,
  and the Word was God.
He was in the beginning with God.
All things came to be through him,
  and without him nothing came to be.
What came to be through him was life,
  and this life was the light of the
      human race;
the light shines in the darkness,
  and the darkness has not overcome it.

A man named John was sent from God. He came for testimony, to testify to the light, so that all might believe through him. He was not the light, but came to testify to the light. The true light, which enlightens everyone, was coming into the world.

He was in the world,
  and the world came to be through him,
  but the world did not know him.
He came to what was his own,
  but his own people did not accept him.

But to those who did accept him he gave power to become children of God, to those who believe in his name, who were born not by natural generation nor by human choice nor by a man's decision but of God.

And the Word became flesh
  and made his dwelling among us,
  and we saw his glory,
  the glory as of the Father's only Son,
  full of grace and truth.

John testified to him and cried out, saying, "This was he of whom I said, 'The one who is coming after me ranks ahead of me because he existed before me.'" From his fullness we have all received, grace in place of grace, because while the law was given through Moses, grace and truth came through Jesus Christ. No one has ever seen God. The only Son, God, who is at the Father's side, has revealed him.

First Reading (Isa 52:7-10)

How beautiful upon the mountains
    are the feet of him who brings glad tidings,
announcing peace, bearing good news,
    announcing salvation, and saying to Zion,
    "Your God is King!"

Hark! Your sentinels raise a cry,
    together they shout for joy,
for they see directly, before their eyes,
    the LORD restoring Zion.
Break out together in song,
    O ruins of Jerusalem!
For the LORD comforts his people,
    he redeems Jerusalem.
The LORD has bared his holy arm
    in the sight of all the nations;
all the ends of the earth will behold
    the salvation of our God.

Responsorial Psalm (Ps 98:1, 2-3, 3-4, 5-6)

R̸. (3c) All the ends of the earth have seen the saving power of God.

Sing to the LORD a new song,
    for he has done wondrous deeds;
his right hand has won victory for him,
    his holy arm.

R̸. All the ends of the earth have seen the saving power of God.

The LORD has made his salvation known:
    in the sight of the nations he has revealed his justice.
He has remembered his kindness and his faithfulness
    toward the house of Israel.

R̸. All the ends of the earth have seen the saving power of God.

All the ends of the earth have seen
    the salvation by our God.
Sing joyfully to the LORD, all you lands;
    break into song; sing praise.

R̸. All the ends of the earth have seen the saving power of God.

Sing praise to the LORD with the harp,
  with the harp and melodious song.
With trumpets and the sound of the horn
  sing joyfully before the King, the LORD.

R̸. All the ends of the earth have seen the saving power of God.

See Appendix, p. 212, for Second Reading

Reflecting on Living the Gospel

On this miraculous Christmas Day we celebrate how God's teaching and revelatory work shifted from telling and showing into doing. Jesus came into the world so that we might encounter God in real time and find our joy and purpose in that union. We, as humans, learn most by doing. And so perhaps we can learn to follow Christ into our ultimate destiny of union with God by doing the things that Jesus showed us how to do.

Making Connections

The words "In the beginning" from today's gospel should sound familiar, as they are the same words from the opening of the book of Genesis. It is sometimes easy to think about our Scripture readings in isolation. Today is an invitation to remember that we read Scripture holistically as a continuous narrative of God's love.

Psalmist Preparation

This psalm's refrain reminds us that God's saving Christmas work is for everyone. "All the ends of the earth" bear witness to and participate in what God wants for us. God wants no less than for us to participate in God's very own life, one that is marked not by the sufferings of this world but by unending love and joy and goodness. We are so deeply loved and desired by one who is so great and powerful. This is the Christmas message, and it is cause for great rejoicing. As you prepare to proclaim this psalm, reflect on what in your own life might be keeping you from participating fully in this joy. Know that God sees and knows whatever pain you are experiencing, and that the God who entered fully into the human experience remains with you in your suffering.

Prayer

God of New Beginnings,
your eternal Word entered human time and space,
announcing to each soul your joy, comfort, and salvation.
All the ends of the earth have seen the saving power of God.
Help us to see your Son's glory, grace, and truth,
he who was and is your Word Incarnate.
Amen.

Gospel (Luke 2:16-21; L18ABC)

The shepherds went in haste to Bethlehem and found Mary and Joseph, and the infant lying in the manger. When they saw this, they made known the message that had been told them about this child. All who heard it were amazed by what had been told them by the shepherds. And Mary kept all these things, reflecting on them in her heart. Then the shepherds returned, glorifying and praising God for all they had heard and seen, just as it had been told to them.

When eight days were completed for his circumcision, he was named Jesus, the name given him by the angel before he was conceived in the womb.

First Reading (Num 6:22-27)

The LORD said to Moses: "Speak to Aaron and his sons and tell them: This is how you shall bless the Israelites. Say to them:

The LORD bless you and keep you!
The LORD let his face shine upon you, and be gracious to you!
The LORD look upon you kindly and give you peace!

So shall they invoke my name upon the Israelites, and I will bless them."

Responsorial Psalm (Ps 67:2-3, 5, 6, 8)

R℣. (2a) May God bless us in his mercy.

May God have pity on us and bless us;
    may he let his face shine upon us.
So may your way be known upon earth;
    among all nations, your salvation.

R℣. May God bless us in his mercy.

May the nations be glad and exult
    because you rule the peoples in equity;
    the nations on the earth you guide.

R℣. May God bless us in his mercy.

May the peoples praise you, O God;
    may all the peoples praise you!
May God bless us,
    and may all the ends of the earth fear him!

R̷. May God bless us in his mercy.

See Appendix, p. 212, for Second Reading

Reflecting on Living the Gospel

The last verse of today's gospel reading is significant, as it proclaims the circumcision and naming of the child Jesus. Every circumcision is a call to Abraham's seed to renew the covenant, but in Jesus, the rite cuts the deepest: the covenant made in his flesh will one day be poured out not only in a drop of foreskin blood, but in his tortured flesh, crucified for the world's salvation. Jesus is given the name that was announced to Mary before his conception (Luke 1:31): "Jesus," which means "savior."

Making Connections

The words with which Aaron blesses the Israelites are fulfilled in the gospel. Now that God is incarnate, God has a face—a literal one. It is shining on us as God-made-flesh takes in the fullness of the human condition and transforms it into something greater. The second reading reminds us that we share in Jesus's status as a child of God; all of us, through him, have received the privilege of calling God our Father.

Psalmist Preparation

This psalm includes the words that God gives to Aaron to use as a blessing. You are blessing the congregation as you sing them. At the same time, you are also *part* of the assembly, singing not "May God bless *you*" but "May God bless *us*." As you prepare this psalm, reflect on your dual role at Mass. You are a full member of the congregation, a full participant in the liturgy, *and* you are a leader amongst the congregation, called forth for a particular role because of your particular gifts. Do you identify with one of these roles more easily than the other?

Prayer

Divine Compassion,
you who free us from our sins
and make us heirs to your love and life,
hear our prayer today: *May God bless us in his mercy.*
Look upon us and bless us;
enter our hearts and dwell within us,
you who are God for ever and ever.
Amen.

Gospel (Matt 2:1-12; L20ABC)

When Jesus was born in Bethlehem of Judea, in the days of King Herod, behold, magi from the east arrived in Jerusalem, saying, "Where is the newborn king of the Jews? We saw his star at its rising and have come to do him homage." When King Herod heard this, he was greatly troubled, and all Jerusalem with him. Assembling all the chief priests and the scribes of the people, he inquired of them where the Christ was to be born. They said to him, "In Bethlehem of Judea, for thus it has been written through the prophet:

And you, Bethlehem, land of Judah,
* are by no means least among the rulers of Judah;*
since from you shall come a ruler,
* who is to shepherd my people Israel."*

Then Herod called the magi secretly and ascertained from them the time of the star's appearance. He sent them to Bethlehem and said, "Go and search diligently for the child. When you have found him, bring me word, that I too may go and do him homage." After their audience with the king they set out. And behold, the star that they had seen at its rising preceded them, until it came and stopped over the place where the child was. They were overjoyed at seeing the star, and on entering the house they saw the child with Mary his mother. They prostrated themselves and did him homage. Then they opened their treasures and offered him gifts of gold, frankincense, and myrrh. And having been warned in a dream not to return to Herod, they departed for their country by another way.

First Reading (Isa 60:1-6)

Rise up in splendor, Jerusalem! Your light has come,
  the glory of the Lord shines upon you.
See, darkness covers the earth,
  and thick clouds cover the peoples;
but upon you the LORD shines,
  and over you appears his glory.
Nations shall walk by your light,
  and kings by your shining radiance.

Raise your eyes and look about;
   they all gather and come to you:
your sons come from afar,
   and your daughters in the arms of their nurses.

Then you shall be radiant at what you see,
   your heart shall throb and overflow,
for the riches of the sea shall be emptied out before you,
   the wealth of nations shall be brought to you.
Caravans of camels shall fill you,
   dromedaries from Midian and Ephah;
all from Sheba shall come
   bearing gold and frankincense,
   and proclaiming the praises of the LORD.

Responsorial Psalm (Ps 72:1-2, 7-8, 10-11, 12-13)

℞. (cf. 11) Lord, every nation on earth will adore you.

O God, with your judgment endow the king,
   and with your justice, the king's son;
he shall govern your people with justice
   and your afflicted ones with judgment.

℞. Lord, every nation on earth will adore you.

Justice shall flower in his days,
   and profound peace, till the moon be no more.
May he rule from sea to sea,
   and from the River to the ends of the earth.

℞. Lord, every nation on earth will adore you.

The kings of Tarshish and the Isles shall offer gifts;
   the kings of Arabia and Seba shall bring tribute.
All kings shall pay him homage,
   all nations shall serve him.

℞. Lord, every nation on earth will adore you.

For he shall rescue the poor when he cries out,
   and the afflicted when he has no one to help him.
He shall have pity for the lowly and the poor;
   the lives of the poor he shall save.

℞. Lord, every nation on earth will adore you.

See Appendix, p. 212, for Second Reading

Reflecting on Living the Gospel

In our Christmas creches, the magi may seem "odd men out" in the humble company of Mary, Joseph, and the child. But with their fine gifts and opulent robes, they do belong there, for they are symbolic of every nation on earth that, in the words of the responsorial Psalm 72, we pray will come to adore God and participate in a kingdom of justice and peace that only God can establish, especially for the poor and needy of the earth.

Making Connections

The gospel has a clear fulfillment of the first reading's prophecy; the magi from faraway lands are following light to Jerusalem. But there is a dark turn; Herod's wicked jealousy makes Jerusalem an unsafe place even for the newborn king, and the magi must move on to Bethlehem as their ultimate destination. Isaiah's prophecy has yet to be achieved in its fullness. Even still, the magi rejoice at what the star reveals to them; even if the story is not yet complete, this is a moment of God's word being fulfilled.

Psalmist Preparation

Happy tongue-twister Sunday! Be proactive in practicing "Tarshish and the Isles" and "nations shall serve" before they trip you up. Note also that this psalm does not just affirm that God is to get worldwide adoration; it also gives a reason that God deserves this. It is God's just and compassionate treatment of the poor and lowly that earns our praise. As part of your preparation with this psalm, could you find a way to participate in bringing about justice for those who are poor? Look for an opportunity for solidarity this week, knowing that God is especially present with those who are afflicted.

Prayer

God, Radiant Splendor,
all peoples bow down before you,
every nation on earth will adore you.
Reveal to us the fullness of your promises,
and show us the ways of your truth.
Shepherd us, keep us safe.
We make this prayer though your son,
Christ, Lord for ever and ever.
Amen.

Gospel (John 1:29-34; L64A)

John the Baptist saw Jesus coming toward him and said, "Behold, the Lamb of God, who takes away the sin of the world. He is the one of whom I said, 'A man is coming after me who ranks ahead of me because he existed before me.' I did not know him, but the reason why I came baptizing with water was that he might be made known to Israel." John testified further, saying, "I saw the Spirit come down like a dove from heaven and remain upon him. I did not know him, but the one who sent me to baptize with water told me, 'On whomever you see the Spirit come down and remain, he is the one who will baptize with the Holy Spirit.' Now I have seen and testified that he is the Son of God."

First Reading (Isa 49:3, 5-6)

The LORD said to me: You are my servant,
    Israel, through whom I show my glory.
Now the LORD has spoken
    who formed me as his servant from the womb,
that Jacob may be brought back to him
    and Israel gathered to him;
and I am made glorious in the sight of the LORD,
    and my God is now my strength!
It is too little, the LORD says, for you to be my servant,
    to raise up the tribes of Jacob,
    and restore the survivors of Israel;
I will make you a light to the nations,
    that my salvation may reach to the ends of the earth.

Responsorial Psalm (Ps 40:2, 4, 7-8, 8-9, 10)

℟. (8a and 9a) Here am I, Lord; I come to do your will.

I have waited, waited for the LORD,
  and he stooped toward me and heard my cry.
And he put a new song into my mouth,
  a hymn to our God.

℟. Here am I, Lord; I come to do your will.

Sacrifice or offering you wished not,
  but ears open to obedience you gave me.
Holocausts or sin-offerings you sought not;
  then said I, "Behold I come."

℟. Here am I, Lord; I come to do your will.

"In the written scroll it is prescribed for me,
to do your will, O my God, is my delight,
  and your law is within my heart!"

℟. Here am I, Lord; I come to do your will.

I announced your justice in the vast assembly;
  I did not restrain my lips, as you, O LORD, know.

℟. Here am I, Lord; I come to do your will.

Second Reading (1 Cor 1:1-3)

Reflecting on Living the Gospel

The readings for this Sunday are rather like a hinged door. The Lectionary pushes it open to allow us to gaze backward at the significant figure of John the Baptist, who points to the One we have celebrated as coming among us in the flesh in the Advent and Christmas seasons. And the readings also direct our gaze forward to our ongoing call to be servants of God among the nations for the long haul of Ordinary Time.

Making Connections

It is easy to see foreshadowing of John the Baptist in Isaiah's reference to himself as one "formed as [God's] servant from the womb." After all, we see John's first moment of action when he leaps in Elizabeth's womb, recognizing Jesus in joy even before either of their faces was visible. The second reading is also about callings, both Paul's particular calling as an apostle and the universal call to holiness that his entire audience—including us—shares.

Psalmist Preparation

We hear this psalm at some big moments in the church year; it is often associated with Mary and proclaimed in conjunction with the annunciation story. But it can also a fitting way to start this new segment of the liturgical calendar. Here, at the beginning of Ordinary Time, we place ourselves in the presence of God; we assume a posture of listening; and we state our intention to live as God wants. As you prepare to proclaim this psalm, think about how God's will has unfolded in your life thus far, and how it is still revealing itself.

Prayer

Servant God,
you who inspire in us a desire to share
your light and your good news,
inspire in us also fervent prayer and patient hearts,
that, when we pray, *"Here am I, Lord; I come to do your will,"*
our desire is sincere and our focus is always you and you alone.
Amen.

Gospel (Matt 4:12-23
[or Matt 4:12-17]; L67A)

When Jesus heard that John had been arrested, he withdrew to Galilee. He left Nazareth and went to live in Capernaum by the sea, in the region of Zebulun and Naphtali, that what had been said through Isaiah the prophet might be fulfilled:

> Land of Zebulun and land
>   of Naphtali,
>   the way to the sea, beyond the
>   Jordan,
>   Galilee of the Gentiles,
> the people who sit in darkness have seen a great light,
> on those dwelling in a land overshadowed by death
>   light has arisen.

From that time on, Jesus began to preach and say, "Repent, for the kingdom of heaven is at hand."

As he was walking by the Sea of Galilee, he saw two brothers, Simon who is called Peter, and his brother Andrew, casting a net into the sea; they were fishermen. He said to them, "Come after me, and I will make you fishers of men." At once they left their nets and followed him. He walked along from there and saw two other brothers, James, the son of Zebedee, and his brother John. They were in a boat, with their father Zebedee, mending their nets. He called them, and immediately they left their boat and their father and followed him. He went around all of Galilee, teaching in their synagogues, proclaiming the gospel of the kingdom, and curing every disease and illness among the people.

First Reading (Isa 8:23–9:3)

First the LORD degraded the land of Zebulun and the land of Naphtali; but in the end he has glorified the seaward road, the land west of the Jordan, the District of the Gentiles.

> Anguish has taken wing, dispelled is darkness:
>   for there is no gloom where but now there was distress.
> The people who walked in darkness
>   have seen a great light;

upon those who dwelt in the land of gloom
    a light has shone.
You have brought them abundant joy
    and great rejoicing,
as they rejoice before you as at the harvest,
    as people make merry when dividing spoils.
For the yoke that burdened them,
    the pole on their shoulder,
and the rod of their taskmaster
    you have smashed, as on the day of Midian.

Responsorial Psalm (Ps 27:1, 4, 13-14)

R︎. (1a) The Lord is my light and my salvation.

The LORD is my light and my salvation;
    whom should I fear?
The LORD is my life's refuge;
    of whom should I be afraid?

R︎. The Lord is my light and my salvation.

One thing I ask of the LORD;
    this I seek:
to dwell in the house of the LORD
    all the days of my life,
that I may gaze on the loveliness of the LORD
    and contemplate his temple.

R︎. The Lord is my light and my salvation.

I believe that I shall see the bounty of the LORD
    in the land of the living.
Wait for the LORD with courage;
    be stouthearted, and wait for the LORD.

R︎. The Lord is my light and my salvation.

Second Reading (1 Cor 1:10-13, 17)

Reflecting on Living the Gospel

As disciples of Jesus we—like Peter and Andrew, James and John—are all called at various times to leave something behind to follow him. We, too, cannot stay put in an immature understanding of Jesus, cannot remain in enterprises that contradict our baptismal calling, or accept social structures that are contrary to the gospel ethic of love and respect for human dignity. Each of us has to name for ourselves, in our own time and place, how we radically turn our hearts to the following of Jesus.

Making Connections

The beginning of Jesus's preaching is the fulfillment of Isaiah's prophecy: Jesus himself is the great light for those who are dwelling in darkness. This must have been evident to Simon, Andrew, James, and John; Jesus's invitation is an odd interruption in their daily work, but they find themselves compelled to drop everything, leave their livelihoods and families behind, and follow him.

Psalmist Preparation

We can imagine the fishermen singing this psalm as they accept Jesus's call; they have identified him as their light and so their fear is cast out as they wholeheartedly choose to follow him. It's okay if you are not able to sing it so wholeheartedly; for most of us the choice to follow Jesus comes gradually, building up through small choices rather than being a once-and-for-all deal. There is much to fear in this world, many reasons to hesitate in giving over our hearts and lives. As you prepare the psalm this week, try to bring your fears and anxieties to Jesus. Know that he sees them, and you, with the utmost love. He does not leave you alone with your fears.

Prayer

God who Rescues,
your light breaks through the gloom
and shines on all with warmth and joy.
Bring each human soul into your luminous presence,
that all may rightly say, *"The Lord is my light and my salvation."*
May your light help us see human divisions
and a clear path to unity and peace.
Amen.

Gospel (Matt 5:1-12a; L70A)

When Jesus saw the crowds, he went up the mountain, and after he had sat down, his disciples came to him. He began to teach them, saying:

"Blessed are the poor in spirit,
for theirs is the kingdom of heaven.
Blessed are they who mourn,
for they will be comforted.
Blessed are the meek,
for they will inherit the land.
Blessed are they who hunger and
thirst for righteousness,
for they will be satisfied.
Blessed are the merciful,
for they will be shown mercy.
Blessed are the clean of heart,
for they will see God.
Blessed are the peacemakers,
for they will be called children of God.
Blessed are they who are persecuted for the sake of righteousness,
for theirs is the kingdom of heaven.
Blessed are you when they insult you and persecute you and utter every kind of evil against you falsely because of me. Rejoice and be glad, for your reward will be great in heaven."

First Reading (Zeph 2:3; 3:12-13)

Seek the Lord, all you humble of the earth,
who have observed his law;
seek justice, seek humility;
perhaps you may be sheltered
on the day of the Lord's anger.

But I will leave as a remnant in your midst
a people humble and lowly,
who shall take refuge in the name of the Lord:
the remnant of Israel.
They shall do no wrong
and speak no lies;

nor shall there be found in their mouths
    a deceitful tongue;
they shall pasture and couch their flocks
    with none to disturb them.

Responsorial Psalm (Ps 146:6-7, 8-9, 9-10)

R℣. (Matt 5:3) Blessed are the poor in spirit; the kingdom of heaven is theirs! *or:* R℣. Alleluia.

The LORD keeps faith forever,
    secures justice for the oppressed,
    gives food to the hungry.
The LORD sets captives free.

R℣. Blessed are the poor in spirit; the kingdom of heaven is theirs!
or: R℣. Alleluia.

The LORD gives sight to the blind;
    the LORD raises up those who were bowed down.
The LORD loves the just;
    the LORD protects strangers.

R℣. Blessed are the poor in spirit; the kingdom of heaven is theirs!
or: R℣. Alleluia.

The fatherless and the widow the LORD sustains,
    but the way of the wicked he thwarts.
The LORD shall reign forever;
    your God, O Zion, through all generations. Alleluia.

R℣. Blessed are the poor in spirit; the kingdom of heaven is theirs!
or: R℣. Alleluia.

Second Reading (1 Cor 1:26-31)

Reflecting on Living the Gospel

The radical significance of what we refer to as "the Beatitudes" can be diluted and sanitized by familiarity. Christian intuition is right to recognize the importance of this text as a program of identity and action for Jesus's disciples, but this has often made it a lifesaving raft to which we cling when unable to think of what gospel passage to use, for example, at a funeral, wedding, or school Mass. In fact, this gospel is dangerous, more like a high-powered motorboat that carries us into deep waters of discipleship.

Making Connections

In the first reading, righteous people are instructed to seek humility. This is a funny command, because it seems that in this life humility often finds us without us trying. We make mistakes often and our very human condition reminds us not to think too highly of ourselves. Humility doesn't always feel good, but it is the thing that saves us; it is one of the many reversals that Jesus preaches. The second reading affirms God's reversal of human values. Those whom the world considers foolish, weak, and lowly are chosen and called by God.

Psalmist Preparation

In this psalm, we hear an affirmation of the gospel's message that God's values are not our own. God's efforts—God's preferential love—are for those who are oppressed, imprisoned, and estranged, those who would be seen as lesser in most societies. As you prepare this psalm, consider your own role in cultures of oppression and injustice. Are there systemic sins from which you have benefited? How might you work to do away with them? Keep these in mind as you proclaim the psalm this week, knowing that the ongoing, tiresome work of fighting off injustice is what puts us on God's side.

Prayer

God of Paradox,
in you there is light in the darkness,
strength in weakness, new life in death.
How *[b]lessed are the poor in spirit; the kingdom of heaven is theirs!*
Help us to love you, your mystery,
your ways which are beyond all human understanding.
Amen.

Gospel (Matt 5:13-16; L73A)

Jesus said to his disciples: "You are the salt of the earth. But if salt loses its taste, with what can it be seasoned? It is no longer good for anything but to be thrown out and trampled underfoot. You are the light of the world. A city set on a mountain cannot be hidden. Nor do they light a lamp and then put it under a bushel basket; it is set on a lampstand, where it gives light to all in the house. Just so, your light must shine before others, that they may see your good deeds and glorify your heavenly Father."

First Reading (Isa 58:7-10)

Thus says the LORD:
   Share your bread with the hungry,
      shelter the oppressed and the homeless;
   clothe the naked when you see them,
      and do not turn your back on your own.
   Then your light shall break forth like the dawn,
      and your wound shall quickly be healed;
   your vindication shall go before you,
      and the glory of the LORD shall be your rear guard.
   Then you shall call, and the LORD will answer,
      you shall cry for help, and he will say: Here I am!
   If you remove from your midst
      oppression, false accusation and malicious speech;
   if you bestow your bread on the hungry
      and satisfy the afflicted;
   then light shall rise for you in the darkness,
      and the gloom shall become for you like midday.

Responsorial Psalm (Ps 112:4-5, 6-7, 8-9)

℟. (4a) The just man is a light in darkness to the upright. *or:* ℟. Alleluia.

Light shines through the darkness for the upright;
he is gracious and merciful and just.
Well for the man who is gracious and lends,
who conducts his affairs with justice.

℟. The just man is a light in darkness to the upright. *or:* ℟. Alleluia.

He shall never be moved;
the just one shall be in everlasting remembrance.
An evil report he shall not fear;
his heart is firm, trusting in the LORD.

℟. The just man is a light in darkness to the upright. *or:* ℟. Alleluia.

His heart is steadfast; he shall not fear.
Lavishly he gives to the poor;
his justice shall endure forever;
his horn shall be exalted in glory.

℟. The just man is a light in darkness to the upright. *or:* ℟. Alleluia.

Second Reading (1 Cor 2:1-5)

Reflecting on Living the Gospel

By calling his disciples "the salt of the earth," Jesus is suggesting they must "savor" the world with God's love, making it more to "God's taste" (see 2 Kgs 2:19-22), healing its wounds. What contemporary corruption must we name and challenge so that our Christian "saltiness" contributes to humanity, society, our church, and our planet being preserved and healed for the kingdom of God? Salt is not sweet and sugary, and neither can our Christian discipleship be. Put salt on a sore spot and it stings as well as heals.

Making Connections

The first reading shares the light imagery of the gospel and gives us more explicit instructions for becoming light to the world. We are to provide food, shelter, and clothing for those in need. In readings of the previous weeks, this has been identified as God's work, as God's special area of interest. When we perform these deeds, we participate in God's preferential love for those who are poor. And we share in the beauty that God is continuously bestowing on the world in God's infinite generosity.

Psalmist Preparation

This psalm echoes the imagery of both gospel and first reading; people who act in justice and generosity are both recipients and conduits of God's very own light. The psalm adds an element of trust, as well; the just one described here is also characterized by steadfastness and trust in God. As you prepare this psalm, think about opportunities you might have to further enact God's justice and goodness in the world. Pray that all in the congregation will act on their own opportunities so that your community might become a beaming source of light for others.

Prayer

God of Justice,
you use each of us, gifted, called, and sent,
to work together in building your reign on earth.
When we do what is just, we are *a light in darkness to the upright.*
Help us to heed the voices of your prophets,
who speak your truth and call us always to greater holiness.
Amen.

Gospel (Matt 5:17-37 [or shorter form below Matt 5:20-22a, 27-28, 33-34a, 37]; L76A)

Jesus said to his disciples: "I tell you, unless your righteousness surpasses that of the scribes and Pharisees, you will not enter the kingdom of heaven.

"You have heard that it was said to your ancestors,

> *You shall not kill; and whoever kills will be liable to judgment.*

But I say to you, whoever is angry with his brother will be liable to judgment.

"You have heard that it was said, *You shall not commit adultery.* But I say to you, everyone who looks at a woman with lust has already committed adultery with her in his heart.

"Again you have heard that it was said to your ancestors,

> *Do not take a false oath,*
> *but make good to the Lord all that you vow.*

But I say to you, do not swear at all. Let your 'Yes' mean 'Yes,' and your 'No' mean 'No.' Anything more is from the evil one."

First Reading (Sir 15:15-20)

If you choose you can keep the commandments, they will save you;
    if you trust in God, you too shall live;
he has set before you fire and water;
    to whichever you choose, stretch forth your hand.
Before man are life and death, good and evil,
    whichever he chooses shall be given him.
Immense is the wisdom of the Lord;
    he is mighty in power, and all-seeing.
The eyes of God are on those who fear him;
    he understands man's every deed.
No one does he command to act unjustly,
    to none does he give license to sin.

Responsorial Psalm (Ps 119:1-2, 4-5, 17-18, 33-34)

℟. (1b) Blessed are they who follow the law of the Lord!

Blessed are they whose way is blameless,
    who walk in the law of the LORD.
Blessed are they who observe his decrees,
    who seek him with all their heart.

℟. Blessed are they who follow the law of the Lord!

You have commanded that your precepts
    be diligently kept.
Oh, that I might be firm in the ways
    of keeping your statutes!

℟. Blessed are they who follow the law of the Lord!

Be good to your servant, that I may live
    and keep your words.
Open my eyes, that I may consider
    the wonders of your law.

℟. Blessed are they who follow the law of the Lord!

Instruct me, O LORD, in the way of your statutes,
    that I may exactly observe them.
Give me discernment, that I may observe your law
    and keep it with all my heart.

℟. Blessed are they who follow the law of the Lord!

Second Reading (1 Cor 2:6-10)

Reflecting on Living the Gospel

Jesus does not come to abolish the Law or the Prophets but to transcend, interiorize, strip away empty externals and legalistic minutiae that had distorted God's revelation. So he focuses not so much on the evils of murder, adultery, or lying, but on the way these take root in the human heart. It's easy to reject the end point of the continuum of evil and yet never recognize the subtle and dangerous first point when we begin to orient our lives in that direction.

Making Connections

The first reading affirms that God's commands are trustworthy and true; obeying them is a source of life and goodness. The Law is not an obligation to be lived in begrudging obedience; it is a gift from God, an assurance that goodness and righteousness are within our reach. The second reading acknowledges that God's wisdom is distinct from human wisdom; it often seems to us to be mysterious and hidden. Even so, it is worthy of trust.

Psalmist Preparation

The psalm states briefly and explicitly what the other readings get at more obliquely: "Open my eyes, that I may consider / the wonders of your law." God's commands sometimes feel like a drudgery because of the consequences of sin, but they are in fact a gift, a gracious revelation that enables us to live wholeheartedly aligned with Christ. As you prepare and proclaim this psalm, consider which moral teachings of the church you struggle with or have struggled with. If we trust that God always wills our good, how might God help you understand these teachings not as an obligation to drudgery but as an invitation to freedom?

Prayer

God of Law, God of Love,
your son, love incarnate, fulfilled the law
and showed us how to live as your people.
Blessed are they who follow the law of the Lord!
Help us to listen for your voice still today,
you who are still speaking, you who are still perfect love.
Amen.

Gospel (Matt 5:38-48; L79A)

Jesus said to his disciples: "You have heard that it was said,

An eye for an eye and a tooth for a tooth.

But I say to you, offer no resistance to one who is evil. When someone strikes you on your right cheek, turn the other one as well. If anyone wants to go to law with you over your tunic, hand over your cloak as well. Should anyone press you into service for one mile, go for two miles. Give to the one who asks of you, and do not turn your back on one who wants to borrow.

"You have heard that it was said,

You shall love your neighbor and hate your enemy.

But I say to you, love your enemies and pray for those who persecute you, that you may be children of your heavenly Father, for he makes his sun rise on the bad and the good, and causes rain to fall on the just and the unjust. For if you love those who love you, what recompense will you have? Do not the tax collectors do the same? And if you greet your brothers only, what is unusual about that? Do not the pagans do the same? So be perfect, just as your heavenly Father is perfect."

First Reading (Lev 19:1-2, 17-18)

The LORD said to Moses, "Speak to the whole Israelite community and tell them: Be holy, for I, the LORD, your God, am holy.

"You shall not bear hatred for your brother or sister in your heart. Though you may have to reprove your fellow citizen, do not incur sin because of him. Take no revenge and cherish no grudge against any of your people. You shall love your neighbor as yourself. I am the LORD."

Responsorial Psalm **(Ps 103:1-2, 3-4, 8, 10, 12-13)**

℟. (8a) The Lord is kind and merciful.

Bless the LORD, O my soul;
   and all my being, bless his holy name.
Bless the LORD, O my soul,
   and forget not all his benefits.

℟. The Lord is kind and merciful.

He pardons all your iniquities,
   heals all your ills.
He redeems your life from destruction,
   crowns you with kindness and compassion.

℟. The Lord is kind and merciful.

Merciful and gracious is the LORD,
   slow to anger and abounding in kindness.
Not according to our sins does he deal with us,
   nor does he requite us according to our crimes.

℟. The Lord is kind and merciful.

As far as the east is from the west,
   so far has he put our transgressions from us.
As a father has compassion on his children,
   so the LORD has compassion on those who fear him.

℟. The Lord is kind and merciful.

Second Reading (1 Cor 3:16-23)

Reflecting on Living the Gospel

God is so generous, and a disciple should be so secure in this love, that there is no need to insist on one's rights. Writing his gospel through the prism of Jesus's death and resurrection, Matthew sees the light of Jesus's response to love broken into the colors of the generous, practical, and radical. For the sake of others, even enemies, Jesus went the "extra mile" to his death, did not retaliate against the blows during his passion, and was stripped, not only of clothes but of life itself.

Making Connections

Jesus's gospel teachings are not the first time God has given commandments to love profoundly: "[L]ove your neighbor as yourself" is already pretty radical. As in the gospel, this love is commanded in imitation of

God; we are to strive for the holiness and perfection that characterizes God's very self. The second reading also reminds us of our dignity and our call to holiness; here, the image of the temple is used to illustrate how God dwells within us. The psalm offers an important counterbalance to the commands of the other readings: even when we fail in our quest for holiness, God is ready to greet us with mercy.

Psalmist Preparation

This psalm offers an important counterbalance to the demands of the gospel. We will often fail in our mission to imitate God's perfection and holiness, but God is infinitely patient with our slow progress, faithfully awaiting us with boundless mercy. As you prepare this psalm, think of a time you have made a misstep in your own journey of holiness. If you have brought this misstep to the sacrament of confession, thank God for the mercy you encountered there. If you have not, make a plan to respond to God's endless invitation to experience that mercy. Either way, say a prayer of thanks to God for the mercy he promises, and bring your gratitude to your proclamation of this psalm.

Prayer

Holy One,
you who *is kind and merciful,*
you teach us to love our neighbors as ourselves,
and to pray for our enemies.
Especially when your lessons are hard,
give to us a spirit of trust and of perseverance,
that we may ever strive to be one holy people,
one in your love and truth.
Amen.

Gospel **(Matt 6:1-6, 16-18; L219)**

Jesus said to his disciples: "Take care not to perform righteous deeds in order that people may see them; otherwise, you will have no recompense from your heavenly Father. When you give alms, do not blow a trumpet before you, as the hypocrites do in the synagogues and in the streets to win the praise of others. Amen, I say to you, they have received their reward. But when you give alms, do not let your left hand know what your right is doing, so that your almsgiving may be secret. And your Father who sees in secret will repay you.

"When you pray, do not be like the hypocrites, who love to stand and pray in the synagogues and on street corners so that others may see them. Amen, I say to you, they have received their reward. But when you pray, go to your inner room, close the door, and pray to your Father in secret. And your Father who sees in secret will repay you.

"When you fast, do not look gloomy like the hypocrites. They neglect their appearance, so that they may appear to others to be fasting. Amen, I say to you, they have received their reward. But when you fast, anoint your head and wash your face, so that you may not appear to be fasting, except to your Father who is hidden. And your Father who sees what is hidden will repay you."

First Reading (Joel 2:12-18)

Even now, says the LORD,
   return to me with your whole heart,
   with fasting, and weeping, and mourning;
Rend your hearts, not your garments,
   and return to the LORD, your God.
For gracious and merciful is he,
   slow to anger, rich in kindness,
   and relenting in punishment.
Perhaps he will again relent
   and leave behind him a blessing,
Offerings and libations
   for the LORD, your God.

Blow the trumpet in Zion!
   proclaim a fast,
   call an assembly;
Gather the people,
   notify the congregation;
Assemble the elders,
   gather the children
   and the infants at the breast;
Let the bridegroom quit his room
   and the bride her chamber.
Between the porch and the altar
   let the priests, the ministers of the LORD, weep,
And say, "Spare, O LORD, your people,
   and make not your heritage a reproach,
   with the nations ruling over them!
Why should they say among the peoples,
   'Where is their God?'"

Then the LORD was stirred to concern for his land and took pity on his people.

Responsorial Psalm (Ps 51:3-4, 5-6ab, 12-13, 14, and 17)

R̊. (see 3a) Be merciful, O Lord, for we have sinned.

Have mercy on me, O God, in your goodness;
   in the greatness of your compassion wipe out my offense.
Thoroughly wash me from my guilt
   and of my sin cleanse me.

R̊. Be merciful, O Lord, for we have sinned.

For I acknowledge my offense,
   and my sin is before me always:
"Against you only have I sinned,
   and done what is evil in your sight."

R̊. Be merciful, O Lord, for we have sinned.

A clean heart create for me, O God,
   and a steadfast spirit renew within me.
Cast me not out from your presence,
   and your Holy Spirit take not from me.

R̊. Be merciful, O Lord, for we have sinned.

Give me back the joy of your salvation,
  and a willing spirit sustain in me.
O Lord, open my lips,
  and my mouth shall proclaim your praise.
℞. Be merciful, O Lord, for we have sinned.

See Appendix, p. 212, for Second Reading

Reflecting on Living the Gospel

Jesus tells listeners to "go to your inner room, close the door, and pray to your Father in secret." This method of prayer enables us to journey to the center of our spirits, the temple in which God dwells in us, and assess whether the structure is sturdy enough to endure the storms of our broken world. Let us go into our inner rooms in humility and with the trust that God will give us what we need to lay a sturdy foundation.

Making Connections

Jesus reminds us in the gospel today that when we pray, fast, and give alms, we do so to grow in relationship with God and others. Prayer, fasting, and almsgiving are not ends in themselves, nor are they about self-centered accolades or self-promotion. May we make this prayer our own and remember that our ministry should always refrain from self-centered attention.

Psalmist Preparation

As we embark on our Lenten practices of repentance, we should know better than to try to do them alone. Prayer, fasting, and almsgiving work to create conditions under which God can operate, but it is always God who does the real work of making us new. This psalm acknowledges this utter dependence on God. We acknowledge our wrongdoings and we profess a commitment to renewal, but ultimately we turn to God because God is the only one who can create clean hearts for us. We ask God not just for a patch job that will cover over the wrongs of the past; we ask for God the Creator to step in and make us anew. This is what God's mercy promises: totally transformative healing that sets us up for fuller freedom going forward.

Prayer

Ever-Present God,
you are constant, you are love,
always awaiting our return to you and your love for us.
Be merciful, O Lord, for we have sinned.
Show us your kindness and truth,
and bring us closer to you and your righteousness.
We make this prayer through Christ our Lord.
Amen.

FEBRUARY 26, 2023

Gospel (Matt 4:1-11; L22A)

At that time Jesus was led by the Spirit into the desert to be tempted by the devil. He fasted for forty days and forty nights, and afterwards he was hungry. The tempter approached and said to him, "If you are the Son of God, command that these stones become loaves of bread." He said in reply, "It is written:

One does not live on bread alone,
but on every word that comes forth
from the mouth of God."

Then the devil took him to the holy city, and made him stand on the parapet of the temple, and said to him, "If you are the Son of God, throw yourself down. For it is written:

He will command his angels concerning you
and with their hands they will support you,
lest you dash your foot against a stone."

Jesus answered him, "Again it is written,

You shall not put the Lord, your God, to the test."

Then the devil took him up to a very high mountain, and showed him all the kingdoms of the world in their magnificence, and he said to him, "All these I shall give to you, if you will prostrate yourself and worship me." At this, Jesus said to him, "Get away, Satan! It is written:

The Lord, your God, shall you worship
and him alone shall you serve."

Then the devil left him and, behold, angels came and ministered to him.

First Reading (Gen 2:7-9; 3:1-7)

The LORD God formed man out of the clay of the ground and blew into his nostrils the breath of life, and so man became a living being.

Then the LORD God planted a garden in Eden, in the east, and placed there the man whom he had formed. Out of the ground the LORD God made various trees grow that were delightful to look at and good for food, with the tree of life in the middle of the garden and the tree of the knowledge of good and evil.

Now the serpent was the most cunning of all the animals that the LORD God had made. The serpent asked the woman, "Did God really tell you not to eat from any of the trees in the garden?" The woman answered the serpent: "We may eat of the fruit of the trees in the garden; it is only about the fruit of the tree in the middle of the garden that God said, 'You shall not eat it or even touch it, lest you die.'" But the serpent said to the woman: "You certainly will not die! No, God knows well that the moment you eat of it your eyes will be opened and you will be like gods who know what is good and what is evil." The woman saw that the tree was good for food, pleasing to the eyes, and desirable for gaining wisdom. So she took some of its fruit and ate it; and she also gave some to her husband, who was with her, and he ate it. Then the eyes of both of them were opened, and they realized that they were naked; so they sewed fig leaves together and made loincloths for themselves.

Responsorial Psalm **(Ps 51:3-4, 5-6, 12-13, 17)**

R̷. (cf. 3a) Be merciful, O Lord, for we have sinned.

Have mercy on me, O God, in your goodness;
  in the greatness of your compassion wipe out my offense.
Thoroughly wash me from my guilt
  and of my sin cleanse me.

R̷. Be merciful, O Lord, for we have sinned.

For I acknowledge my offense,
  and my sin is before me always:
"Against you only have I sinned,
  and done what is evil in your sight."

R̷. Be merciful, O Lord, for we have sinned.

A clean heart create for me, O God,
  and a steadfast spirit renew within me.
Cast me not out from your presence,
  and your Holy Spirit take not from me.

R̷. Be merciful, O Lord, for we have sinned.

Give me back the joy of your salvation,
  and a willing spirit sustain in me.
O Lord, open my lips,
  and my mouth shall proclaim your praise.
℟. Be merciful, O Lord, for we have sinned.

See Appendix, p. 213, for Second Reading

Reflecting on Living the Gospel

The tempter puts Jesus to the test three times in a verbal battle where the word of God is misused by Satan and used correctly and faithfully by Jesus. By putting nothing but the words of the Hebrew Scriptures on Jesus's lips, Matthew witnesses to us that the word of God is a "sword of the Spirit" (Eph 6:17) in the fight against temptation. Matthew is not concerned with how Jesus thought of himself, but with how the Christians of his and future Christian communities would think about Jesus.

Making Connections

Jesus's response to the devil stands in contrast to Adam and Eve's; he outsmarts temptation at every turn where their naivete caused them to cave immediately. Unfortunately, this is not enough to undo the consequences of sin; this work will be continued all the way to Calvary. The second reading affirms Jesus as the mirror image of Adam. Through Adam we inherit sin and death; from Jesus we inherit freedom and life.

Psalmist Preparation

Our sin is a sure thing; thankfully, so is God's mercy. The joy of Lent is often hidden beneath its solemn tone of repentance, but this psalm reveals its secret. We have sinned, yes, and this is cause for sorrow; but the psalm ends with us returning to praise. Lenten work is not about taking on sacrifice for its own sake, but about enabling God to continue the work of creation and renewal that God loves to do. We ask God to return us to "the joy of salvation," and we can rest assured that God wants to do so. Can you infuse your Lenten practices with joy? Does this change your attitude toward the season?

Prayer

Creator God,
you made everything good and holy.
Sometimes we stray from your path,
tempted by this world's desires.
Be merciful, O Lord, for we have sinned.
Help us recognize the gift of Jesus Christ,
the pinnacle of your creation,
and his sacrifice, his salvation, his grace.
Amen.

Gospel (Matt 17:1-9; L25A)

Jesus took Peter, James, and John his brother, and led them up a high mountain by themselves. And he was transfigured before them; his face shone like the sun and his clothes became white as light. And behold, Moses and Elijah appeared to them, conversing with him. Then Peter said to Jesus in reply, "Lord, it is good that we are here. If you wish, I will make three tents here, one for you, one for Moses, and one for Elijah." While he was still speaking, behold, a bright cloud cast a shadow over them, then from the cloud came a voice that said, "This is my be-

loved Son, with whom I am well pleased; listen to him." When the disciples heard this, they fell prostrate and were very much afraid. But Jesus came and touched them, saying, "Rise, and do not be afraid." And when the disciples raised their eyes, they saw no one else but Jesus alone.

As they were coming down from the mountain, Jesus charged them, "Do not tell the vision to anyone until the Son of Man has been raised from the dead."

First Reading (Gen 12:1-4a)

The LORD said to Abram: "Go forth from the land of your kinsfolk and from your father's house to a land that I will show you.

"I will make of you a great nation,
    and I will bless you;
I will make your name great,
    so that you will be a blessing.
I will bless those who bless you
    and curse those who curse you.
All the communities of the earth
    shall find blessing in you."

Abram went as the LORD directed him.

Responsorial Psalm (Ps 33:4-5, 18-19, 20, 22)

℟. (22) Lord, let your mercy be on us, as we place our trust in you.

Upright is the word of the LORD,
  and all his works are trustworthy.
He loves justice and right;
  of the kindness of the LORD the earth is full.

℟. Lord, let your mercy be on us, as we place our trust in you.

See, the eyes of the LORD are upon those who fear him,
  upon those who hope for his kindness,
to deliver them from death
  and preserve them in spite of famine.

℟. Lord, let your mercy be on us, as we place our trust in you.

Our soul waits for the LORD,
  who is our help and our shield.
May your kindness, O LORD, be upon us
  who have put our hope in you.

℟. Lord, let your mercy be on us, as we place our trust in you.

See Appendix, p. 213, for Second Reading

Reflecting on Living the Gospel

Peter, James, and John witness the glory of Jesus's transfiguration. Then, as a sign of the transfiguration to come, Jesus touches these disciples of his and raises them from their fear—fear of what might be the implications of this mountain revelation for themselves. Then they see "no one except Jesus" on the mountain. For all disciples in every age, he is the one whom we must trust to grasp us, raise us up from our fears, and lead us into the new.

Making Connections

Like the disciples in the gospel, Abram receives explicit directions from God. He does not respond in fear but in trust, immediately fulfilling the instructions he receives. His life of love and obedience prepares him to respond when God asks something big of him. The second reading affirms the role of the transfiguration. Along with the entire life of Jesus, the transfiguration makes manifest the grace of God, which has been with us all along.

Psalmist Preparation

Like last week's psalm, this one pairs God's mercy and our trust. The two go together. God deserves our trust because God is trustworthy; his unfailing offer of unconditional love enables us to draw ever closer to him despite our ongoing failings. At the same time, the last stanza of this psalm reminds us that God does not often work on the timeline we choose. We often find ourselves waiting for God's voice and God's healing. As you prepare this psalm, think of an area of your life where you find yourself waiting for God. Strive to wait with trust rather than impatience.

Prayer

Divine Providence,
you are with all pilgrims who journey to you, with you,
a guiding light for sinners who seek you.
[L]et your mercy be on us, as we place our trust in you.
Guide us, give to us a glimpse of a future with you,
filled with hope, joy, and promise.
Amen.

Gospel (John 4:5-42
[or shorter form below John 4:5-15, 19b-26,
39a, 40-42]; L28A)

Jesus came to a town of Samaria called
Sychar, near the plot of land that Jacob had
given to his son Joseph. Jacob's well was
there. Jesus, tired from his journey, sat down
there at the well. It was about noon.

A woman of Samaria came to draw water.
Jesus said to her, "Give me a drink." His disciples had gone into the town to buy food. The
Samaritan woman said to him, "How can you,
a Jew, ask me, a Samaritan woman, for a drink?" —For Jews use nothing in
common with Samaritans.— Jesus answered and said to her, "If you knew
the gift of God and who is saying to you, 'Give me a drink,' you would have
asked him and he would have given you living water." The woman said to
him, "Sir, you do not even have a bucket and the cistern is deep; where then
can you get this living water? Are you greater than our father Jacob, who
gave us this cistern and drank from it himself with his children and his
flocks?" Jesus answered and said to her, "Everyone who drinks this water
will be thirsty again; but whoever drinks the water I shall give will never
thirst; the water I shall give will become in him a spring of water welling up
to eternal life." The woman said to him, "Sir, give me this water, so that I
may not be thirsty or have to keep coming here to draw water."

"Sir, I can see that you are a prophet. Our ancestors worshiped on this
mountain; but you people say that the place to worship is in Jerusalem."
Jesus said to her, "Believe me, woman, the hour is coming when you will
worship the Father neither on this mountain nor in Jerusalem. You people
worship what you do not understand; we worship what we understand, because salvation is from the Jews. But the hour is coming, and is now here,
when true worshipers will worship the Father in Spirit and truth; and indeed
the Father seeks such people to worship him. God is Spirit, and those who
worship him must worship in Spirit and truth." The woman said to him, "I
know that the Messiah is coming, the one called the Christ; when he comes,
he will tell us everything." Jesus said to her, "I am he, the one who is speaking with you."

Many of the Samaritans of that town began to believe in him. When
the Samaritans came to him, they invited him to stay with them; and he
stayed there two days. Many more began to believe in him because of his

word, and they said to the woman, "We no longer believe because of your word; for we have heard for ourselves, and we know that this is truly the savior of the world."

First Reading (Exod 17:3-7)

In those days, in their thirst for water, the people grumbled against Moses, saying, "Why did you ever make us leave Egypt? Was it just to have us die here of thirst with our children and our livestock?" So Moses cried out to the LORD, "What shall I do with this people? A little more and they will stone me!" The LORD answered Moses, "Go over there in front of the people, along with some of the elders of Israel, holding in your hand, as you go, the staff with which you struck the river. I will be standing there in front of you on the rock in Horeb. Strike the rock, and the water will flow from it for the people to drink." This Moses did, in the presence of the elders of Israel. The place was called Massah and Meribah, because the Israelites quarreled there and tested the LORD, saying, "Is the LORD in our midst or not?"

Responsorial Psalm (Ps 95:1-2, 6-7, 8-9)

R̸. (8) If today you hear his voice, harden not your hearts.

Come, let us sing joyfully to the LORD;
    let us acclaim the Rock of our salvation.
Let us come into his presence with thanksgiving;
    let us joyfully sing psalms to him.

R̸. If today you hear his voice, harden not your hearts.

Come, let us bow down in worship;
    let us kneel before the LORD who made us.
For he is our God,
    and we are the people he shepherds, the flock he guides.

R̸. If today you hear his voice, harden not your hearts.

Oh, that today you would hear his voice:
    "Harden not your hearts as at Meribah,
    as in the day of Massah in the desert,
where your fathers tempted me;
    they tested me though they had seen my works."

R̸. If today you hear his voice, harden not your hearts.

See Appendix, p. 213, for Second Reading

Reflecting on Living the Gospel

Jesus makes those who respond to him sharers in his freedom. The despised woman of today's gospel, who comes to the well in the heat of high noon to avoid the judgmental eyes and tongues of the other women, hurries back to her own town. She is no longer ashamed of the story of her life because she has a more urgent story to tell about the man who lowered a bucket into the well of her soul and drew up the deep living water within her.

Making Connections

The first reading shares the strong water imagery of the gospel; God provides for us in all ways, including our very human need for water. Our physical thirst reveals the neediness of our human condition; it is never satisfied for long, and we must stay close enough to a source of water to constantly fulfill a need that was satisfied not long ago. The second reading is more oblique, but does speak of the love of God being "poured out" into our hearts—an indication that physical thirst is neither our primary need nor the primary way that God provides.

Psalmist Preparation

Most of us assume that when we hear God's voice, we'll be ready to listen. Surely it's God's uncommunicativeness that's the issue, not our ability to hear him! But this psalm reminds us that our hearts need to stay open in order to keep hearing God. God is always reaching out to us, but often in ways we miss because we're not expecting them. As part of your preparation to proclaim this psalm, spend some time in silence. Ask God to reveal to you one place you've been overlooking God's presence in your life. Pray for a softer heart so that you might more readily notice God in all the gentle ways God comes to us.

Prayer

Living Water,
you accompany us in all life's trials,
refreshing and enlivening weary souls.
Your voice bids us *"harden not your hearts,"*
lest we never come to drink
from your living spring of eternal life.
Help us receive you and your graces
with a willing, receptive heart.
Amen.

Gospel (John 9:1-41 [or shorter form below John 9:1, 6-9, 13-17, 34-38]; L31A)

As Jesus passed by he saw a man blind from birth. He spat on the ground and made clay with the saliva, and smeared the clay on his eyes, and said to him, "Go wash in the Pool of Siloam"—which means Sent—. So he went and washed, and came back able to see.

His neighbors and those who had seen him earlier as a beggar said, "Isn't this the one who used to sit and beg?" Some said, "It is," but others said, "No, he just looks like him." He said, "I am."

They brought the one who was once blind to the Pharisees. Now Jesus had made clay and opened his eyes on a sabbath. So then the Pharisees also asked him how he was able to see. He said to them, "He put clay on my eyes, and I washed, and now I can see." So some of the Pharisees said, "This man is not from God, because he does not keep the sabbath." But others said, "How can a sinful man do such signs?" And there was a division among them. So they said to the blind man again, "What do you have to say about him, since he opened your eyes?" He said, "He is a prophet."

They answered and said to him, "You were born totally in sin, and are you trying to teach us?" Then they threw him out.

When Jesus heard that they had thrown him out, he found him and said, "Do you believe in the Son of Man?" He answered and said, "Who is he, sir, that I may believe in him?" Jesus said to him, "You have seen him, and the one speaking with you is he." He said, "I do believe, Lord," and he worshiped him.

First Reading (1 Sam 16:1b, 6-7, 10-13a)

The LORD said to Samuel: "Fill your horn with oil, and be on your way. I am sending you to Jesse of Bethlehem, for I have chosen my king from among his sons."

As Jesse and his sons came to the sacrifice, Samuel looked at Eliab and thought, "Surely the LORD's anointed is here before him." But the LORD said to Samuel: "Do not judge from his appearance or from his lofty

stature, because I have rejected him. Not as man sees does God see, because man sees the appearance but the LORD looks into the heart."
In the same way Jesse presented seven sons before Samuel, but Samuel said to Jesse, "The LORD has not chosen any one of these." Then Samuel asked Jesse, "Are these all the sons you have?" Jesse replied, "There is still the youngest, who is tending the sheep." Samuel said to Jesse, "Send for him; we will not begin the sacrificial banquet until he arrives here." Jesse sent and had the young man brought to them. He was ruddy, a youth handsome to behold and making a splendid appearance. The LORD said, "There—anoint him, for this is the one!" Then Samuel, with the horn of oil in hand, anointed David in the presence of his brothers; and from that day on, the spirit of the LORD rushed upon David.

Responsorial Psalm (Ps 23:1-3a, 3b-4, 5, 6)

℟. (1) The Lord is my shepherd; there is nothing I shall want.

The LORD is my shepherd; I shall not want.
  In verdant pastures he gives me repose;
beside restful waters he leads me;
  he refreshes my soul.

℟. The Lord is my shepherd; there is nothing I shall want.

He guides me in right paths
  for his name's sake.
Even though I walk in the dark valley
  I fear no evil; for you are at my side
with your rod and your staff
  that give me courage.

℟. The Lord is my shepherd; there is nothing I shall want.

You spread the table before me
  in the sight of my foes;
you anoint my head with oil;
  my cup overflows.

℟. The Lord is my shepherd; there is nothing I shall want.

Only goodness and kindness follow me
  all the days of my life;
and I shall dwell in the house of the LORD
  for years to come.

℟. The Lord is my shepherd; there is nothing I shall want.

See Appendix, p. 213, for Second Reading

Reflecting on Living the Gospel

Today's gospel challenges us, as individuals and communities, to examine how we see with the eyes of faith and whether we are willfully blind to the Sent One, turning away from the Light of the World. What are our contemporary blindnesses? Sin gets clicks. Are we more interested in sin than in grace? Are we brave enough to accept being sometimes ostracized by others when we choose to walk in the light of Christ rather than stumble away from him along our complacent, selfish, and socially pressurized paths of darkness?

Making Connections

The first reading contains a much more mundane form of blindness. Jesse merely *overlooks* David, assuming his youngest son cannot be the one chosen by God. But God is clear that his perception is not the same as ours; what God values is not the same as what we value. The second reading continues the themes of light and darkness, exhorting us to choose light over darkness—which is to say, sight over blindness.

Psalmist Preparation

Shepherds were not people of prominence in the ancient world; shepherding was dirty, smelly, humble work. It would not have been immediately obvious that identifying God as a shepherd was a form of praise. Like our other readings, this psalm is about defying expectations; the shepherd here provides such tender care that gratitude spills forth as praise. This psalm can sometimes feel mind-numbingly familiar. When was the last time you really tried to pray with it? Spend some time with it this week as you prepare to proclaim it and ask God to make it new for you.

Prayer

Healing Presence,
you anoint all who live in pain and distress,
and guide all to wholeness and boundless, restorative love.
You are *my shepherd; there is nothing I shall want.*
Open our eyes, open our hearts,
that all may truly see you, know you, and love you in return.
Amen.

Gospel (John 11:1-45 [or shorter form below John 11:3-7, 17, 20-27, 33b-45]; L34A)

The sisters of Lazarus sent word to Jesus saying, "Master, the one you love is ill." When Jesus heard this he said, "This illness is not to end in death, but is for the glory of God, that the Son of God may be glorified through it." Now Jesus loved Martha and her sister and Lazarus. So when he heard that he was ill, he remained for two days in the place where he was. Then after this he said to his disciples, "Let us go back to Judea."

When Jesus arrived, he found that Lazarus had already been in the tomb for four days. When Martha heard that Jesus was coming, she went to meet him; but Mary sat at home. Martha said to Jesus, "Lord, if you had been here, my brother would not have died. But even now I know that whatever you ask of God, God will give you." Jesus said to her, "Your brother will rise." Martha said, "I know he will rise, in the resurrection on the last day." Jesus told her, "I am the resurrection and the life; whoever believes in me, even if he dies, will live, and everyone who lives and believes in me will never die. Do you believe this?" She said to him, "Yes, Lord. I have come to believe that you are the Christ, the Son of God, the one who is coming into the world."

He became perturbed and deeply troubled, and said, "Where have you laid him?" They said to him, "Sir, come and see." And Jesus wept. So the Jews said, "See how he loved him." But some of them said, "Could not the one who opened the eyes of the blind man have done something so that this man would not have died?"

So Jesus, perturbed again, came to the tomb. It was a cave, and a stone lay across it. Jesus said, "Take away the stone." Martha, the dead man's sister, said to him, "Lord, by now there will be a stench; he has been dead for four days." Jesus said to her, "Did I not tell you that if you believe you will see the glory of God?" So they took away the stone. And Jesus raised his eyes and said, "Father, I thank you for hearing me. I know that you always hear me; but because of the crowd here I have said this, that they may believe that you sent me." And when he had said this, he cried out in a loud voice, "Lazarus, come out!" The dead man came out, tied hand and foot with burial bands, and his face was wrapped in a cloth. So Jesus said to them, "Untie him and let him go."

Now many of the Jews who had come to Mary and seen what he had done began to believe in him.

First Reading (Ezek 37:12-14)

Thus says the Lord GOD: O my people, I will open your graves and have you rise from them, and bring you back to the land of Israel. Then you shall know that I am the LORD, when I open your graves and have you rise from them, O my people! I will put my spirit in you that you may live, and I will settle you upon your land; thus you shall know that I am the LORD. I have promised, and I will do it, says the LORD.

Responsorial Psalm (Ps 130:1-2, 3-4, 5-6, 7-8)

R̸. (7) With the Lord there is mercy and fullness of redemption.

Out of the depths I cry to you, O LORD;
    LORD, hear my voice!
Let your ears be attentive
    to my voice in supplication.

R̸. With the Lord there is mercy and fullness of redemption.

If you, O LORD, mark iniquities,
    LORD, who can stand?
But with you is forgiveness,
    that you may be revered.

R̸. With the Lord there is mercy and fullness of redemption.

I trust in the LORD;
    my soul trusts in his word.
More than sentinels wait for the dawn,
    let Israel wait for the LORD.

R̸. With the Lord there is mercy and fullness of redemption.

For with the LORD is kindness
    and with him is plenteous redemption;
and he will redeem Israel
    from all their iniquities.

R̸. With the Lord there is mercy and fullness of redemption.

See Appendix, p. 214, for Second Reading

Reflecting on Living the Gospel

Today's gospel proclaims that no one is so far gone into death that Jesus cannot call him or her back to life, for he *is* the resurrection and the life, which is more than just physical life. John 11 is both a touchingly human narrative and a profound theological statement. Now as then, Jesus knows our struggles, will stand by the grave of our dead hopes, will weep with us in our pain and loss, and will reveal to us the glory of God that frees us from death.

Making Connections

In the first reading, God reveals through Ezekiel that death does not have the final say. Despite death's appearance of permanence, God's power is greater still, and what God wants for us is life. The second reading affirms that while our bodies still die, this is no longer the end it once was. Christ's Spirit living in us allows us to share in his triumph over death.

Psalmist Preparation

We begin to see in this gospel the "fullness of redemption" promised in the psalm. Jesus's work of healing the sick and blind has all been a prelude to this, the restoration of life even to those who are dead. And so, as the psalm affirms, we trust in the Lord, waiting to experience the fullness of life he promises. As you prepare this psalm, think about ways you are still waiting for God to work in your life. Bring something specific to your proclamation of the psalm and make it an earnest prayer of trust.

Prayer

God of Promises,
you who raise the dead to new life,
you who cry with us, and set us free:
with you *there is mercy and fullness of redemption.*
Fill us with your spirit, know of our trust,
and redeem us, O holy Son of God.
Amen.

Gospel at the procession with palms
(Matt 21:1-11; L37A)

Gospel at Mass **(Matt 26:14–27:66
[or 27:11-54]; L38A)**

First Reading **(Isa 50:4-7)**

The Lord God has given me
    a well-trained tongue,
that I might know how to speak to the
      weary
    a word that will rouse them.
Morning after morning
    he opens my ear that I may hear;
and I have not rebelled,
    have not turned back.
I gave my back to those who beat me,
    my cheeks to those who plucked my beard;
my face I did not shield
    from buffets and spitting.

The Lord God is my help,
    therefore I am not disgraced;
I have set my face like flint,
    knowing that I shall not be put to shame.

Responsorial Psalm **(Ps 22:8-9, 17-18, 19-20, 23-24)**

℟. (2a) My God, my God, why have you abandoned me?
All who see me scoff at me;
    they mock me with parted lips, they wag their heads:
"He relied on the Lord; let him deliver him,
    let him rescue him, if he loves him."

℟. My God, my God, why have you abandoned me?
Indeed, many dogs surround me,
    a pack of evildoers closes in upon me;
they have pierced my hands and my feet;
    I can count all my bones.

℟. My God, my God, why have you abandoned me?

They divide my garments among them,
  and for my vesture they cast lots.
But you, O LORD, be not far from me;
  O my help, hasten to aid me.

R̸. My God, my God, why have you abandoned me?

I will proclaim your name to my brethren;
  in the midst of the assembly I will praise you:
"You who fear the LORD, praise him;
  all you descendants of Jacob, give glory to him;
  revere him, all you descendants of Israel!"

R̸. My God, my God, why have you abandoned me?

See Appendix, p. 214, for Second Reading

Reflecting on Living the Gospel

Throughout this entire passion narrative, with its many characters, including some regarded today as saints, only Pilate's wife honestly intervenes to try to save Jesus. Just as Matthew's infancy narrative had dreamers like Joseph and the magi, so here is another dreamer. But a woman's dreams and witness are unacceptable. Pilate washes his hands of the whole dirty matter. Compromise, dismissal of the "dreams" of others, peer pressure, and fear of losing upward social mobility: these can also send our truth as followers of Jesus gurgling down the drain.

Making Connections

The first reading provides the first moment of stark contrast between the procession's triumphant tones and the gravity of the passion. The glory of Jesus's entrance into Jerusalem was not for its own sake. The beautiful hymn of the second reading captures this paradox in all its fullness: Jesus shares God's being by rights, but by choice humbles himself to death. It is this humility that allows his even greater exaltation and the worship we now bring to the one who gives us life.

Psalmist Preparation

This psalm is heart wrenching but relatable. All of us, at some moment in our lives of faith, will feel that we have been abandoned by God. The demands of faith do not always reward us with warm feelings that reassure us of God's presence and approval. But at the end of this psalm the writer issues a reminder: even without those pleasant feelings, we can still praise the God who deserves our trust even when all seems lost. This is the God who brings life out of death itself. As you prepare this psalm, think of a time you have felt abandoned by God. Ask God to show you how God was present in that time.

Prayer

God of the Lost,
at times it is hard to know your presence,
when life overwhelms and shadows hide your face.
In these times, hear our cries:
My God, my God, why have you abandoned me?
Help us know you are always with us,
abiding in patient support, gentle love, and everlasting life.
Amen.

Gospel (John 13:1-15; L39ABC)

Before the feast of Passover, Jesus knew that his hour had come to pass from this world to the Father. He loved his own in the world and he loved them to the end. The devil had already induced Judas, son of Simon the Iscariot, to hand him over. So, during supper, fully aware that the Father had put everything into his power and that he had come from God and was returning to God, he rose from supper and took off his outer garments. He took a towel and tied it around his waist. Then he poured water into a basin and began

to wash the disciples' feet and dry them with the towel around his waist. He came to Simon Peter, who said to him, "Master, are you going to wash my feet?" Jesus answered and said to him, "What I am doing, you do not understand now, but you will understand later." Peter said to him, "You will never wash my feet." Jesus answered him, "Unless I wash you, you will have no inheritance with me." Simon Peter said to him, "Master, then not only my feet, but my hands and head as well." Jesus said to him, "Whoever has bathed has no need except to have his feet washed, for he is clean all over; so you are clean, but not all." For he knew who would betray him; for this reason, he said, "Not all of you are clean."

So when he had washed their feet and put his garments back on and reclined at table again, he said to them, "Do you realize what I have done for you? You call me 'teacher' and 'master,' and rightly so, for indeed I am. If I, therefore, the master and teacher, have washed your feet, you ought to wash one another's feet. I have given you a model to follow, so that as I have done for you, you should also do."

First Reading (Exod 12:1-8, 11-14)

The LORD said to Moses and Aaron in the land of Egypt, "This month shall stand at the head of your calendar; you shall reckon it the first month of the year. Tell the whole community of Israel: On the tenth of this month every one of your families must procure for itself a lamb, one apiece for each household. If a family is too small for a whole lamb, it shall join the nearest household in procuring one and shall share in the lamb in proportion to the number of persons who partake of it. The lamb must be a year-old male and without blemish. You may take it from either the sheep or the goats. You shall keep it until the fourteenth day of this month, and then, with the whole assembly of Israel present, it shall be slaughtered during the evening twilight. They shall take some of its blood and apply it to the two doorposts and the lintel of every house in which they partake of the lamb. That same night they shall eat its roasted flesh with unleavened bread and bitter herbs.

"This is how you are to eat it: with your loins girt, sandals on your feet and your staff in hand, you shall eat like those who are in flight. It is the Passover of the LORD. For on this same night I will go through Egypt, striking down every firstborn of the land, both man and beast, and executing judgment on all the gods of Egypt—I, the LORD! But the blood will mark the houses where you are. Seeing the blood, I will pass over you; thus, when I strike the land of Egypt, no destructive blow will come upon you.

"This day shall be a memorial feast for you, which all your generations shall celebrate with pilgrimage to the LORD, as a perpetual institution."

Responsorial Psalm (Ps 116:12-13, 15-16bc, 17-18)

R̲7. (cf. 1 Cor 10:16) Our blessing-cup is a communion with the Blood of Christ.

How shall I make a return to the LORD
    for all the good he has done for me?
The cup of salvation I will take up,
    and I will call upon the name of the LORD.

R̲7. Our blessing-cup is a communion with the Blood of Christ.

Precious in the eyes of the LORD
    is the death of his faithful ones.
I am your servant, the son of your handmaid;
    you have loosed my bonds.

R̲7. Our blessing-cup is a communion with the Blood of Christ.

To you will I offer sacrifice of thanksgiving,
    and I will call upon the name of the LORD.
My vows to the LORD I will pay
    in the presence of all his people.

R̲7. Our blessing-cup is a communion with the Blood of Christ.

HOLY THURSDAY EVENING MASS OF THE LORD'S SUPPER

See Appendix, p. 214, for Second Reading

Reflecting on Living the Gospel

Why proclaim the story of Jesus washing his disciples' feet on the night we remember the institution of the Eucharist? Perhaps, like John's community at the end of the first century, we are used to celebrating Eucharist, but familiarity may have eroded its meaning for us. John reminds us by the washing of the feet, this "parable in action," that Jesus is Servant, one who is ready to do the dirty jobs, to be at the bottom of the social heap, and that following him means being there, too.

Making Connections

Today's celebration reminds us that the Eucharist is more than a personal relationship with Jesus Christ. Rather, Eucharist is the communal act of living for others, following the example of Christ's *agapic*, self-giving love.

Psalmist Preparation

This psalm expresses beautifully what we do at every Mass. We take up the cup of salvation; we offer sacrifice; we call upon the name of God. All of this is done in thanksgiving for all the goodness God continuously offers us. On this evening, when we celebrate the institution of the Eucharist, the psalm reminds us that the very word Eucharist means "thanksgiving." All that we do in liturgy is a response of gratitude to the God who gives us everything. As you prepare to proclaim this psalm, spend some time cultivating gratitude for the particulars of your life and your faith journey. Perhaps take note of one way God has walked with you this Lent, or make a list of gifts you encountered today that you might have taken for granted. Bring your gratitude for these things into your proclamation of this psalm.

Prayer

Servant God,
you show us that to love is to serve,
and that unity with you is sacrifice.
Our blessing-cup is a communion with the blood of Christ.
As you drank the cup, let us also,
that in your blood we may come to know
your radical self-emptying love.
Amen.

Gospel (John 18:1–19:42; L40ABC)

First Reading (Isa 52:13–53:12)

> See, my servant shall prosper,
>> he shall be raised high and greatly
>>> exalted.
> Even as many were amazed at him—
>> so marred was his look beyond
>>> human semblance
> and his appearance beyond that of
>> the sons of man—
> so shall he startle many nations,
>> because of him kings shall stand
>>> speechless;
> for those who have not been told shall see,
>> those who have not heard shall ponder it.

> Who would believe what we have heard?
>> To whom has the arm of the LORD been revealed?
> He grew up like a sapling before him,
>> like a shoot from the parched earth;
> there was in him no stately bearing to make us look at him,
>> nor appearance that would attract us to him.
> He was spurned and avoided by people,
>> a man of suffering, accustomed to infirmity,
> one of those from whom people hide their faces,
>> spurned, and we held him in no esteem.

> Yet it was our infirmities that he bore,
>> our sufferings that he endured,
> while we thought of him as stricken,
>> as one smitten by God and afflicted.
> But he was pierced for our offenses,
>> crushed for our sins;
> upon him was the chastisement that makes us whole,
>> by his stripes we were healed.
> We had all gone astray like sheep,
>> each following his own way;
> but the LORD laid upon him
>> the guilt of us all.

Though he was harshly treated, he submitted
  and opened not his mouth;
like a lamb led to the slaughter
  or a sheep before the shearers,
  he was silent and opened not his mouth.
Oppressed and condemned, he was taken away,
  and who would have thought any more of his destiny?
When he was cut off from the land of the living,
  and smitten for the sin of his people,
a grave was assigned him among the wicked
  and a burial place with evildoers,
though he had done no wrong
  nor spoken any falsehood.
But the Lord was pleased
  to crush him in infirmity.

If he gives his life as an offering for sin,
  he shall see his descendants in a long life,
  and the will of the Lord shall be accomplished through him.

Because of his affliction
  he shall see the light
    in fullness of days;
through his suffering, my servant shall justify many,
  and their guilt he shall bear.
Therefore I will give him his portion among the great,
  and he shall divide the spoils with the mighty,
because he surrendered himself to death
  and was counted among the wicked;
and he shall take away the sins of many,
  and win pardon for their offenses.

Responsorial Psalm (Ps 31:2, 6, 12-13, 15-16, 17, 25)

℟. (Luke 23:46) Father, into your hands I commend my spirit.

In you, O Lord, I take refuge;
  let me never be put to shame.
In your justice rescue me.
Into your hands I commend my spirit;
  you will redeem me, O Lord, O faithful God.

℟. Father, into your hands I commend my spirit.

For all my foes I am an object of reproach,
  a laughingstock to my neighbors, and a dread to my friends;
  they who see me abroad flee from me.
I am forgotten like the unremembered dead;
  I am like a dish that is broken.

R̶7. Father, into your hands I commend my spirit.

But my trust is in you, O LORD;
  I say, "You are my God.
In your hands is my destiny; rescue me
  from the clutches of my enemies and my persecutors."

R̶7. Father, into your hands I commend my spirit.

Let your face shine upon your servant;
  save me in your kindness.
Take courage and be stouthearted,
  all you who hope in the LORD.

R̶7. Father, into your hands I commend my spirit.

See Appendix, p. 215, for Second Reading

Reflecting on Living the Gospel

In John's account of Jesus's death, there is no agonized dying cry, only the silent triumph of one who has accomplished that for which he came into the world. As his final dispossession, Jesus hands over his last breath to his Father, the breath that animates the new creation. No bones of this Paschal Lamb are broken, but from Jesus's pierced side flow blood and water, signs of Eucharist and baptism through which all people can enter into the new temple of the body of the Crucified and Risen One.

Making Connections

Why would a God of love force God's own son to die? Theologian Elizabeth Johnson argues that Jesus died because he proclaimed the kingdom of God, a challenging, even unnerving concept of radical service and kinship that many were unwilling to accept. Jesus was killed because of his commitment to justice and inclusion. Jesus was killed because he called others to conversion. This lens helps us better understand a potentially disturbing reality.

Psalmist Preparation

This is a psalm Jesus quotes from the cross, calling to mind not only the depths of its pain but the heights of its trust. The one who wrote this psalm knew deep and real heartbreak: in the ancient world, it was understood that the dead lived on by being remembered, so the unremembered dead would have been seen to have died a double death. But this is not a psalm of despair. It does not end with Psalm 88's "my only friend is darkness" but with an exhortation to courage and hope. Whatever pain you are experiencing in your own life, bring it to your proclamation of this psalm. Know that you are not alone in your suffering; Jesus sees and knows it and will not leave you alone in it.

Prayer

God, Silenced for Us,
your passion and death teach us
that our words mean nothing if not lived,
and that our lives must take as example
your sacrifice, your everlasting covenant.
May then our only words today be these:
into your hands I commend my spirit.
Bring us into greater union with you.
Amen.

APRIL 8, 2023

Additional readings can be found in the Lectionary for Mass.

Gospel (Matt 28:1-10; L41ABC)

After the sabbath, as the first day of the week was dawning, Mary Magdalene and the other Mary came to see the tomb. And behold, there was a great earthquake; for an angel of the Lord descended from heaven, approached, rolled back the stone, and sat upon it. His appearance was like lightning and his clothing was white as snow. The guards were shaken with fear of him and became like dead men. Then the angel said to the women in reply, "Do not be afraid! I know that you are seeking Jesus the crucified. He is not here, for he has been raised just as he said. Come and see the place where he lay. Then go quickly and tell his disciples, 'He has been raised from the dead, and he is going before you to Galilee; there you will see him.' Behold, I have told you." Then they went away quickly from the tomb, fearful yet overjoyed, and ran to announce this to his disciples. And behold, Jesus met them on their way and greeted them. They approached, embraced his feet, and did him homage. Then Jesus said to them, "Do not be afraid. Go tell my brothers to go to Galilee, and there they will see me."

Epistle (Rom 6:3-11)

Brothers and sisters: Are you unaware that we who were baptized into Christ Jesus were baptized into his death? We were indeed buried with him through baptism into death, so that, just as Christ was raised from the dead by the glory of the Father, we too might live in newness of life.

For if we have grown into union with him through a death like his, we shall also be united with him in the resurrection. We know that our old self was crucified with him, so that our sinful body might be done away with, that we might no longer be in slavery to sin. For a dead person has been absolved from sin. If, then, we have died with Christ, we believe that we shall also live with him. We know that Christ, raised from the dead, dies no more; death no longer has power over him. As to his death, he died to sin once and for all; as to his life, he lives for God. Consequently, you too must think of yourselves as being dead to sin and living for God in Christ Jesus.

Responsorial Psalm (Ps 118:1-2, 16-17, 22-23)

R̦. Alleluia, alleluia, alleluia.

Give thanks to the Lord, for he is good,
for his mercy endures forever.
Let the house of Israel say,
"His mercy endures forever."

R̦. Alleluia, alleluia, alleluia.

"The right hand of the Lord has struck with power;
the right hand of the Lord is exalted.
I shall not die, but live,
and declare the works of the Lord."

R̦. Alleluia, alleluia, alleluia.

The stone which the builders rejected
has become the cornerstone.
By the Lord has this been done;
it is wonderful in our eyes.

R̦. Alleluia, alleluia, alleluia.

Reflecting on Living the Gospel

The risen Jesus announces to the women that his disciples are to meet him in Galilee—Galilee of the springtime of their call, where the winter of their infidelity will thaw in the warmth of the forgiving love of their risen Master, who will commission them to make disciples of all nations. Like they did, we often fail; but we're called back to "Galilee" again and again, called to leave the place of the dead and follow Jesus who offers us his new life. For this, we sing "Alleluia!"

Making Connections

In today's gospel, the women were the first to hear and proclaim the resurrection of Jesus. Unfortunately, when they tried to share this news with others, their story was deemed "nonsense." Whose stories do we deem as nonsense in our own lives today? Which voices do we ignore or disregard? Do we listen to the voices of women, of people of color, of the LGBTQ community, among so many others? As ministers we must tune our ears and hearts to the voices of all we encounter and serve. We see this in the Scripture readings tonight, all of which tell the story of God's relationship with God's people.

Psalmist Preparation

Whichever psalm (or psalms) you are proclaiming tonight, be sure to include a prayerful reflection on its preceding reading as part of your preparation. Different psalms might take on different tones as the story progresses; this extended Liturgy of the Word includes a broad range of emotion before we burst into the first Alleluias of Easter. But note also the theme of God's fidelity that weaves through all these readings; we celebrate on this night that ours is a God who keeps promises. Alleluia indeed.

Prayer

Living, Risen Lord,
death is defeated, the grave is conquered!
There is no greater good news than this!
May our gratitude know no bounds,
and with zeal and sacred fervor may we always proclaim:
Alleluia! Give thanks to the Lord for he is good!
Love is living, now and forever!
Amen.

Gospel (John 20:1-9; L42ABC)

On the first day of the week, Mary of
Magdala came to the tomb early in the
morning, while it was still dark, and saw
the stone removed from the tomb. So she
ran and went to Simon Peter and to the
other disciple whom Jesus loved, and told
them, "They have taken the Lord from the
tomb, and we don't know where they put
him." So Peter and the other disciple went
out and came to the tomb. They both ran,
but the other disciple ran faster than
Peter and arrived at the tomb first; he
bent down and saw the burial cloths

there, but did not go in. When Simon Peter arrived after him, he went
into the tomb and saw the burial cloths there, and the cloth that had
covered his head, not with the burial cloths but rolled up in a separate
place. Then the other disciple also went in, the one who had arrived at
the tomb first, and he saw and believed. For they did not yet understand
the Scripture that he had to rise from the dead.

or Gospel (Matt 28:1-10; L41A)

or at an afternoon or evening Mass
Gospel (Luke 24:13-35; L46)

First Reading (Acts 10:34a, 37-43)

Peter proceeded to speak and said: "You know what has happened all over
Judea, beginning in Galilee after the baptism that John preached, how
God anointed Jesus of Nazareth with the Holy Spirit and power. He went
about doing good and healing all those oppressed by the devil, for God
was with him. We are witnesses of all that he did both in the country of
the Jews and in Jerusalem. They put him to death by hanging him on a
tree. This man God raised on the third day and granted that he be visible,
not to all the people, but to us, the witnesses chosen by God in advance,
who ate and drank with him after he rose from the dead. He commissioned us to preach to the people and testify that he is the one appointed
by God as judge of the living and the dead. To him all the prophets bear
witness, that everyone who believes in him will receive forgiveness of
sins through his name."

Responsorial Psalm **(Ps 118:1-2, 16-17, 22-23)**

R⃥. (24) This is the day the Lord has made; let us rejoice and be glad.
or: R⃥. Alleluia.

Give thanks to the Lord, for he is good,
    for his mercy endures forever.
Let the house of Israel say,
    "His mercy endures forever."

R⃥. This is the day the Lord has made; let us rejoice and be glad.
or: R⃥. Alleluia.

"The right hand of the Lord has struck with power;
    the right hand of the Lord is exalted.
I shall not die, but live,
    and declare the works of the Lord."

R⃥. This is the day the Lord has made; let us rejoice and be glad.
or: R⃥. Alleluia.

The stone which the builders rejected
    has become the cornerstone.
By the Lord has this been done;
    it is wonderful in our eyes.

R⃥. This is the day the Lord has made; let us rejoice and be glad.
or: R⃥. Alleluia.

See Appendix, p. 215, for Second Reading

Reflecting on Living the Gospel

This is the day on which we celebrate not only the resurrection of Christ's body and his triumph over death, but also the resurrection of hope. It is a beautiful aspect of our human nature that we are so often driven to return, to strive, to persist, and to care even against all odds. Let us nurture the hope that lives within our hearts while also placing our trust and our joy in the resurrection God has in store for us—whatever its form.

Making Connections

Rather than climbing the ladder of power, prestige, and wealth, Christ invites us to lower ourselves, embrace humility, and give of ourselves for others. We encounter this in a special way on Easter Sunday, as we are reminded that power comes from sacrifice, that honor comes from humility, and that life comes from death. This is what Peter means in the reading from the Acts of the Apostles when he proclaims, "We are witnesses of all that he did." May we witness to Christ's paschal mystery by living the self-giving love to which we are called.

Psalmist Preparation

"This is the day the Lord has made" can be a confusing sentiment, for God of course makes and gives us every day. But what is always true is more profoundly and clearly true on Easter. On Easter we catch a first glimpse of what God intended from the beginning: human participation in God's own enduring life. We are still awaiting the fullest iteration of this, but today we celebrate what God has already done for us. Sin has been conquered; the battle is won. Death will no more interrupt the goodness God has in store for us. Today we rejoice and are glad.

Prayer

Cornerstone of Life,
risen from the dead, marvelous to behold:
This is the day the Lord has made; let us rejoice and be glad.
You are hope incarnate, reigning forever;
you are redemption, you are healing,
you are forgiveness.
Help us build upon you a life of holiness and love.
Alleluia!
Amen.

Gospel (John 20:19-31; L43A)

On the evening of that first day of the week, when the doors were locked, where the disciples were, for fear of the Jews, Jesus came and stood in their midst and said to them, "Peace be with you." When he had said this, he showed them his hands and his side. The disciples rejoiced when they saw the Lord. Jesus said to them again, "Peace be with you. As the Father has sent me, so I send you." And when he had said this, he breathed on them and said to them, "Receive the Holy Spirit. Whose sins you forgive are forgiven them, and whose sins you retain are retained."

Thomas, called Didymus, one of the Twelve, was not with them when Jesus came. So the other disciples said to him, "We have seen the Lord." But he said to them, "Unless I see the mark of the nails in his hands and put my finger into the nailmarks and put my hand into his side, I will not believe."

Now a week later his disciples were again inside and Thomas was with them. Jesus came, although the doors were locked, and stood in their midst and said, "Peace be with you." Then he said to Thomas, "Put your finger here and see my hands, and bring your hand and put it into my side, and do not be unbelieving, but believe." Thomas answered and said to him, "My Lord and my God!" Jesus said to him, "Have you come to believe because you have seen me? Blessed are those who have not seen and have believed."

Now Jesus did many other signs in the presence of his disciples that are not written in this book. But these are written that you may come to believe that Jesus is the Christ, the Son of God, and that through this belief you may have life in his name.

First Reading (Acts 2:42-47)

They devoted themselves to the teaching of the apostles and to the communal life, to the breaking of bread and to the prayers. Awe came upon everyone, and many wonders and signs were done through the apostles. All who believed were together and had all things in common; they would sell their property and possessions and divide them among all according to each one's need. Every day they devoted themselves to meeting together in the temple area and to breaking bread in their homes. They ate their meals with exultation and sincerity of heart, praising God and enjoying favor with all the people. And every day the Lord added to their number those who were being saved.

Responsorial Psalm (Ps 118:2-4, 13-15, 22-24)

R̸. (1) Give thanks to the Lord for he is good, his love is everlasting.
or: R̸. Alleluia.

Let the house of Israel say,
    "His mercy endures forever."
Let the house of Aaron say,
    "His mercy endures forever."
Let those who fear the LORD say,
    "His mercy endures forever."

R̸. Give thanks to the Lord for he is good, his love is everlasting.
or: R̸. Alleluia.

I was hard pressed and was falling,
    but the LORD helped me.
My strength and my courage is the LORD,
    and he has been my savior.
The joyful shout of victory
    in the tents of the just.

R̸. Give thanks to the Lord for he is good, his love is everlasting.
or: R̸. Alleluia.

The stone which the builders rejected
    has become the cornerstone.
By the LORD has this been done;
    it is wonderful in our eyes.
This is the day the LORD has made;
    let us be glad and rejoice in it.

R̸. Give thanks to the Lord for he is good, his love is everlasting.
or: R̸. Alleluia.

See Appendix, p. 215, for Second Reading

Reflecting on Living the Gospel

For future generations of disciples like ourselves, who will listen to the gospel in the presence of the physically absent Jesus, the Lord pronounces the last beatitude and the one that is our greatest hope: "Blessed are those who have not seen and have believed."

Jesus is still offering us his wounded hands and side. Both individually (like Thomas) and as communities (like the Easter eve gathering), we are being called to recognize him in the wounded ones of our world and in our own wounds.

Making Connections

The gospel tells the story of one of the first encounters with the risen Christ; the first reading tells us about a community living in the wake of such an encounter. They respond to the gospel with awe and generosity, with prayer and communal living. The second reading is written to a community slightly more removed from immediately witnessing the resurrection; while they (and we) need to rely on the testimony of others, it affirms that joy and hope are at the heart of their response.

Psalmist Preparation

This psalm connects Easter back to Lent, thrice repeating that "His mercy endures forever." The sheer, wholehearted rejoicing of this psalm still reminds us that God is working in unexpected ways, for it is the stone rejected by the builders that God chooses as the cornerstone. God's ways continue not to be our ways, but in the light of Easter we see more clearly that God's ways are better. As you prepare this psalm, make a list of five wonderful things in your life. Bring your gratitude for these things to your proclamation, letting your joy for them spill out into an invitation to share that joy.

Prayer

Ever-living God,
your son conquered death
that he might be mercy for a thousand generations.
Be our help when we fail, our strength in our weakness,
and a loving presence in our doubts.
[G]ive thanks to the Lord for he is good, his love is everlasting.
Help our unbelief, hold us close.
Amen.

Gospel (Luke 24:13-35; L46A)

That very day, the first day of the week, two of Jesus' disciples were going to a village seven miles from Jerusalem called Emmaus, and they were conversing about all the things that had occurred. And it happened that while they were conversing and debating, Jesus himself drew near and walked with them, but their eyes were prevented from recognizing him. He asked them, "What are you discussing as you walk along?" They stopped, looking downcast. One of them, named Cleopas, said to him in reply, "Are you the only

visitor to Jerusalem who does not know of the things that have taken place there in these days?" And he replied to them, "What sort of things?" They said to him, "The things that happened to Jesus the Nazarene, who was a prophet mighty in deed and word before God and all the people, how our chief priests and rulers both handed him over to a sentence of death and crucified him. But we were hoping that he would be the one to redeem Israel; and besides all this, it is now the third day since this took place. Some women from our group, however, have astounded us: they were at the tomb early in the morning and did not find his body; they came back and reported that they had indeed seen a vision of angels who announced that he was alive. Then some of those with us went to the tomb and found things just as the women had described, but him they did not see." And he said to them, "Oh, how foolish you are! How slow of heart to believe all that the prophets spoke! Was it not necessary that the Christ should suffer these things and enter into his glory?" Then beginning with Moses and all the prophets, he interpreted to them what referred to him in all the Scriptures. As they approached the village to which they were going, he gave the impression that he was going on farther. But they urged him, "Stay with us, for it is nearly evening and the day is almost over." So he went in to stay with them. And it happened that, while he was with them at table, he took bread, said the blessing, broke it, and gave it to them. With that their eyes were opened and they recognized him, but he vanished from their sight. Then they said to each other, "Were not our hearts burning within us while he spoke to us on the way and opened the Scriptures to us?" So they set out at once and returned to Jerusalem where they found gathered together the eleven and those with them who were saying, "The Lord has truly been raised and has appeared to Simon!" Then the two recounted what had taken place on the way and how he was made known to them in the breaking of bread.

First Reading (Acts 2:14, 22-33)

Then Peter stood up with the Eleven, raised his voice, and proclaimed: "You who are Jews, indeed all of you staying in Jerusalem. Let this be known to you, and listen to my words. You who are Israelites, hear these words. Jesus the Nazorean was a man commended to you by God with mighty deeds, wonders, and signs, which God worked through him in your midst, as you yourselves know. This man, delivered up by the set plan and foreknowledge of God, you killed, using lawless men to crucify him. But God raised him up, releasing him from the throes of death, because it was impossible for him to be held by it. For David says of him:

I saw the Lord ever before me,
with him at my right hand I shall not be disturbed.
Therefore my heart has been glad and my tongue has exulted;
my flesh, too, will dwell in hope,
because you will not abandon my soul to the netherworld,
nor will you suffer your holy one to see corruption.
You have made known to me the paths of life;
you will fill me with joy in your presence.

"My brothers, one can confidently say to you about the patriarch David that he died and was buried, and his tomb is in our midst to this day. But since he was a prophet and knew that God had sworn an oath to him that he would set one of his descendants upon his throne, he foresaw and spoke of the resurrection of the Christ, that neither was he abandoned to the netherworld nor did his flesh see corruption. God raised this Jesus; of this we are all witnesses. Exalted at the right hand of God, he received the promise of the Holy Spirit from the Father and poured him forth, as you see and hear."

Responsorial Psalm (Ps 16:1-2, 5, 7-8, 9-10, 11)

℞. (11a) Lord, you will show us the path of life. *or:* ℞. Alleluia.

Keep me, O God, for in you I take refuge;
   I say to the LORD, "My Lord are you."
O LORD, my allotted portion and my cup,
   you it is who hold fast my lot.

℞. Lord, you will show us the path of life. *or:* ℞. Alleluia.

I bless the LORD who counsels me;
   even in the night my heart exhorts me.
I set the LORD ever before me;
   with him at my right hand I shall not be disturbed.

℞. Lord, you will show us the path of life. *or:* ℞. Alleluia.

Therefore my heart is glad and my soul rejoices,
   my body, too, abides in confidence;
because you will not abandon my soul to the netherworld,
   nor will you suffer your faithful one to undergo corruption.

℞. Lord, you will show us the path of life. *or:* ℞. Alleluia.

You will show me the path to life,
   abounding joy in your presence,
   the delights at your right hand forever.

℞. Lord, you will show us the path of life. *or:* ℞. Alleluia.

See Appendix, p. 215, for Second Reading

Reflecting on Living the Gospel

For Luke, Easter day is filled with action. The women go to the tomb; they announce the resurrection to the Eleven. Peter goes to the tomb but comes away unsure what he has seen. Two disciples leave Jerusalem and head for Emmaus. It is a day of journeying, a day that illustrates that with Jesus we are a pilgrim people. The Emmaus event is about being "on the road," about the new things that we are called to do after we have heard the story of the risen Christ.

Making Connections

The first reading shows Peter in his redemption arc—after his cowardly denial of Jesus in the passion narrative, he here stands up and proclaims the truth of Jesus's life, death, and resurrection. He is ready to take a risk because his encounter with the risen Jesus has transformed him; this courage comes from God. The second reading continues his preaching and reminds us of the source of his courage, a courage that would enable him to follow Jesus to a death by crucifixion: this is not human courage, but courage that only comes when our "faith and hope are in God."

Psalmist Preparation

This psalm's path imagery pairs perfectly with today's gospel, where the disciples encounter Jesus while walking. Journeys and pathways are common imagery for life with God; "walking with God" is a favorite image of the Old Testament for those who lived faithfully. This psalm has a pondering quality, affirming the deep, true ways that God remains with us even if it is not always evident. If you are able, consider praying with this text while walking sometime this week. Reflect on your own journey of faith and the times that God has shown you the path. Remember that some choices God leaves to us, and even when God does not give clear or obvious signposts, God promises to be with us on whatever path we choose.

Prayer

Divine Revelation,
you journey with us always,
making known your presence and sustaining us
with your word and with the gift of yourself.
When we are discouraged, disheartened,
whenever we need your help,
Lord, you will show us the path of life.
Make our hearts burn with your love.
Amen.

Gospel (John 10:1-10; L49A)

Jesus said: "Amen, amen, I say to you, whoever does not enter a sheepfold through the gate but climbs over elsewhere is a thief and a robber. But whoever enters through the gate is the shepherd of the sheep. The gatekeeper opens it for him, and the sheep hear his voice, as the shepherd calls his own sheep by name and leads them out. When he has driven out all his own, he walks ahead of them, and the sheep follow him, because they recognize his voice. But they will not follow a stranger;  they will run away from him, because they do not recognize the voice of strangers." Although Jesus used this figure of speech, the Pharisees did not realize what he was trying to tell them.

So Jesus said again, "Amen, amen, I say to you, I am the gate for the sheep. All who came before me are thieves and robbers, but the sheep did not listen to them. I am the gate. Whoever enters through me will be saved, and will come in and go out and find pasture. A thief comes only to steal and slaughter and destroy; I came so that they might have life and have it more abundantly."

First Reading (Acts 2:14a, 36-41)

Then Peter stood up with the Eleven, raised his voice, and proclaimed: "Let the whole house of Israel know for certain that God has made both Lord and Christ, this Jesus whom you crucified."

Now when they heard this, they were cut to the heart, and they asked Peter and the other apostles, "What are we to do, my brothers?" Peter said to them, "Repent and be baptized, every one of you, in the name of Jesus Christ for the forgiveness of your sins; and you will receive the gift of the Holy Spirit. For the promise is made to you and to your children and to all those far off, whomever the Lord our God will call." He testified with many other arguments, and was exhorting them, "Save yourselves from this corrupt generation." Those who accepted his message were baptized, and about three thousand persons were added that day.

Responsorial Psalm (Ps 23:1-3a, 3b-4, 5, 6)

℟. (1) The Lord is my shepherd; there is nothing I shall want.
or: ℟. Alleluia.

The LORD is my shepherd; I shall not want.
    In verdant pastures he gives me repose;
beside restful waters he leads me;
    he refreshes my soul.

℟. The Lord is my shepherd; there is nothing I shall want.
or: ℟. Alleluia.

He guides me in right paths
    for his name's sake.
Even though I walk in the dark valley
    I fear no evil; for you are at my side
with your rod and your staff
    that give me courage.

℟. The Lord is my shepherd; there is nothing I shall want.
or: ℟. Alleluia.

You spread the table before me
    in the sight of my foes;
you anoint my head with oil;
    my cup overflows.

℟. The Lord is my shepherd; there is nothing I shall want.
or: ℟. Alleluia.

Only goodness and kindness follow me
    all the days of my life;
and I shall dwell in the house of the LORD
    for years to come.

℟. The Lord is my shepherd; there is nothing I shall want.
or: ℟. Alleluia.

See Appendix, p. 216, for Second Reading

Reflecting on Living the Gospel

Peter burns hotly with Pentecost fire in the first reading today, as he proclaims to the crowds of Jerusalem that salvation comes through the Shepherd whose body was ravaged on the cross and who rose again as Lord and Christ of God. Their response to his words is a question from the heart: "What are we to do?"

Is the Pentecost fire still contagious, so that people ask us, "What are we to do?" Perhaps the interest in the Rite of Christian Initiation (RCIA) in our parishes is an indicator?

Making Connections

The second reading explicitly repeats the sheep and shepherd image of the gospel; sheep sometimes go astray but returning to their shepherd keeps them safe. Peter's preaching of baptism in the first reading is an important connection to the sheepfold gate of the gospel. Baptism is how we share in Christ's death and thus his life. It is our entry point to the safety of Christ's flock.

Psalmist Preparation

This psalm can sometimes feel blunted by familiarity; it comes up frequently in the liturgical year, plus it is ubiquitous on wall plaques and throw pillows, sometimes to the point of watering down its beautiful and powerful imagery of God as our shepherd. If you find your eyes glazing over at this psalm, try to spend some time with it in imaginative prayer. Really bring to life the scenes it paints, including what each of your five senses would experience if you were in the loving care of God as described here. When you proclaim the psalm, strive to do so with tender gratitude, knowing that God cares for each member of the congregation this dearly.

Prayer

Sacred Gate of Life,
through you is heaven, and union with the divine.
You guard our coming and going,
keeping us safe, granting abundant life to each human soul.
Each human heart knows you,
each voice lifts their thanks and praise:
You are *my shepherd; there is nothing I shall want.*
Amen.

Gospel (John 14:1-12; L52A)

Jesus said to his disciples: "Do not let your hearts be troubled. You have faith in God; have faith also in me. In my Father's house there are many dwelling places. If there were not, would I have told you that I am going to prepare a place for you? And if I go and prepare a place for you, I will come back again and take you to myself, so that where I am you also may be. Where I am going you know the way." Thomas said to him, "Master, we do not know where you are going; how can we know the way?" Jesus said to him, "I am the way and the truth and the life. No one

comes to the Father except through me. If you know me, then you will also know my Father. From now on you do know him and have seen him." Philip said to him, "Master, show us the Father, and that will be enough for us." Jesus said to him, "Have I been with you for so long a time and you still do not know me, Philip? Whoever has seen me has seen the Father. How can you say, 'Show us the Father'? Do you not believe that I am in the Father and the Father is in me? The words that I speak to you I do not speak on my own. The Father who dwells in me is doing his works. Believe me that I am in the Father and the Father is in me, or else, believe because of the works themselves. Amen, amen, I say to you, whoever believes in me will do the works that I do, and will do greater ones than these, because I am going to the Father."

First Reading (Acts 6:1-7)

As the number of disciples continued to grow, the Hellenists complained against the Hebrews because their widows were being neglected in the daily distribution. So the Twelve called together the community of the disciples and said, "It is not right for us to neglect the word of God to serve at table. Brothers, select from among you seven reputable men, filled with the Spirit and wisdom, whom we shall appoint to this task, whereas we shall devote ourselves to prayer and to the ministry of the word." The proposal was acceptable to the whole community, so they chose Stephen, a man filled with faith and the Holy Spirit, also Philip, Prochorus, Nicanor, Timon, Parmenas, and Nicholas of Antioch, a convert to Judaism. They presented these men to the apostles who prayed and laid hands on them. The word of God continued to spread, and the number of the disciples in Jerusalem increased greatly; even a large group of priests were becoming obedient to the faith.

Responsorial Psalm (Ps 33:1-2, 4-5, 18-19)

℟. (22) Lord, let your mercy be on us, as we place our trust in you.
or: ℟. Alleluia.

Exult, you just, in the LORD;
   praise from the upright is fitting.
Give thanks to the LORD on the harp;
   with the ten-stringed lyre chant his praises.

℟. Lord, let your mercy be on us, as we place our trust in you.
or: ℟. Alleluia.

Upright is the word of the LORD,
   and all his works are trustworthy.
He loves justice and right;
   of the kindness of the LORD the earth is full.

℟. Lord, let your mercy be on us, as we place our trust in you.
or: ℟. Alleluia.

See, the eyes of the LORD are upon those who fear him,
   upon those who hope for his kindness,
to deliver them from death
   and preserve them in spite of famine.

℟. Lord, let your mercy be on us, as we place our trust in you.
or: ℟. Alleluia.

See Appendix, p. 216, for Second Reading

Reflecting on Living the Gospel

Thomas's question haunts us. "Master, we do not know where you are going; how can we know the way?" In even the most faithful life, there may come a time when we seem either to stumble suddenly into darkness or gradually wander away from old certainties. We would all like a simple, clearly marked road to direct us to the Father's house through what is often the dark wood of our lives. What we are offered is not a map but a *person*, Jesus Christ.

Making Connections

Like the gospel, the second reading calls us to follow in Christ's footsteps. Here, we are to follow him in becoming "living stones" that might be built into a "spiritual house." This house is akin to the temple, a place for offering sacrifice. But it can also serve as shelter for others. The first reading reminds us that part of the work of the church is to distribute goods in a just way. This is so important that a new group is established: deacons are initiated to oversee the social work of the church.

Psalmist Preparation

The psalm reflects the shift of the other readings this week, moving from early Easter's wholehearted outpouring of praise to late Easter's re-assurances that our trust in God remains well-founded even as we wait for the work of Easter to be seen in all its fullness. As in Lent, we have a psalm that pairs mercy and trust. We know that God will not abandon us, and we rejoice in that truth. As you prepare this psalm, think about times you have found God to be trustworthy. What is a time when God's promises were fulfilled for you? Bring your gratitude for that moment to your proclamation of this psalm.

Prayer

Way, Truth, and Life,
guiding beacon and gracious consoler:
you are the one true path and one true destination.
At times we stray from you, human weakness prevails.
Lord, let your mercy be on us, as we place our trust in you.
Show us divine love, and we shall be saved.
Amen.

Gospel (John 14:15-21; L55A)

Jesus said to his disciples: "If you love me, you will keep my commandments. And I will ask the Father, and he will give you another Advocate to be with you always, the Spirit of truth, whom the world cannot accept, because it neither sees nor knows him. But you know him, because he remains with you, and will be in you. I will not leave you orphans; I will come to you. In a little while the world will no longer see me, but you will see me, because I live and you will live. On that day you will realize that I am in my Father and you are in me and I in you. Whoever has my commandments and observes them is the one who loves me. And whoever loves me will be loved by my Father, and I will love him and reveal myself to him."

First Reading (Acts 8:5-8, 14-17)

Philip went down to the city of Samaria and proclaimed the Christ to them. With one accord, the crowds paid attention to what was said by Philip when they heard it and saw the signs he was doing. For unclean spirits, crying out in a loud voice, came out of many possessed people, and many paralyzed or crippled people were cured. There was great joy in that city.

Now when the apostles in Jerusalem heard that Samaria had accepted the word of God, they sent them Peter and John, who went down and prayed for them, that they might receive the Holy Spirit, for it had not yet fallen upon any of them; they had only been baptized in the name of the Lord Jesus. Then they laid hands on them and they received the Holy Spirit.

Responsorial Psalm (Ps 66:1-3, 4-5, 6-7, 16, 20)

R℔. (1) Let all the earth cry out to God with joy. *or:* R℔. Alleluia.

Shout joyfully to God, all the earth,
    sing praise to the glory of his name;
    proclaim his glorious praise.
Say to God, "How tremendous are your deeds!"

R℔. Let all the earth cry out to God with joy. *or:* R℔. Alleluia.

"Let all on earth worship and sing praise to you,
    sing praise to your name!"
Come and see the works of God,
    his tremendous deeds among the children of Adam.

℟. Let all the earth cry out to God with joy. *or:* ℟. Alleluia.

He has changed the sea into dry land;
    through the river they passed on foot;
    therefore let us rejoice in him.
He rules by his might forever.

℟. Let all the earth cry out to God with joy. *or:* ℟. Alleluia.

Hear now, all you who fear God, while I declare
    what he has done for me.
Blessed be God who refused me not
    my prayer or his kindness!

℟. Let all the earth cry out to God with joy. *or:* ℟. Alleluia.

See Appendix, p. 216, for Second Reading

Reflecting on Living the Gospel

"We must be still and still moving / Into another intensity / For a further union, a deeper communion."

The poet T. S. Eliot wrote these words in his *Four Quartets*. The communion that we hear proclaimed in today's gospel is the deepest, most intense, and most personal of unions, expressed in Jesus's repeated use of the word *in*. The union is the indwelling of the Paraclete "in you" (meaning Jesus's disciples); of Jesus "in my Father"; of the disciples who are gathered "you in me and I in you."

Making Connections

In the first reading, we see an affirmation of the gospel's idea of the Holy Spirit as an ongoing presence with us beyond Christ's bodily presence on earth. This is depicted in a forerunner of what we now know as the sacrament of confirmation. Those who have been baptized in Samaria have their baptisms completed in a sense when the apostles lay hands on them and the Holy Spirit descends.

Psalmist Preparation

Last week's psalm was a throwback to Lenten themes of God's mercy and our need for patient trust; this one returns to the fullness of Easter rejoicing. The Holy Spirit's ongoing presence, promised in the gospel and demonstrated in the first reading, is reason for a renewed outpouring of gratitude and thanksgiving. As you prepare this psalm, spend some time reflecting on the role of the Holy Spirit in your life; think especially about the gifts of the Spirit (wisdom, understanding, counsel, fortitude, knowledge, piety, and fear of the Lord) and how they play a role in seeing you through the challenges of the life of faith.

Prayer

Mighty Healer, Eternal Love,
your Spirit is among us, within us,
restoring those in need of wholeness,
uplifting those who have fallen.
Let all the earth cry out to God with joy.
You never abandon us, your adopted children,
but always show us your love,
a revelation of life and truth.
Amen.

Gospel (Matt 28:16-20; L58A)

The eleven disciples went to Galilee, to the mountain to which Jesus had ordered them. When they saw him, they worshiped, but they doubted. Then Jesus approached and said to them, "All power in heaven and on earth has been given to me. Go, therefore, and make disciples of all nations, baptizing them in the name of the Father, and of the Son, and of the Holy Spirit, teaching them to observe all that I have commanded you. And behold, I am with you always, until the end of the age."

First Reading (Acts 1:1-11)

In the first book, Theophilus, I dealt with all that Jesus did and taught until the day he was taken up, after giving instructions through the Holy Spirit to the apostles whom he had chosen. He presented himself alive to them by many proofs after he had suffered, appearing to them during forty days and speaking about the kingdom of God. While meeting with them, he enjoined them not to depart from Jerusalem, but to wait for "the promise of the Father about which you have heard me speak; for John baptized with water, but in a few days you will be baptized with the Holy Spirit."

When they had gathered together they asked him, "Lord, are you at this time going to restore the kingdom to Israel?" He answered them, "It is not for you to know the times or seasons that the Father has established by his own authority. But you will receive power when the Holy Spirit comes upon you, and you will be my witnesses in Jerusalem, throughout Judea and Samaria, and to the ends of the earth." When he had said this, as they were looking on, he was lifted up, and a cloud took him from their sight. While they were looking intently at the sky as he was going, suddenly two men dressed in white garments stood beside them. They said, "Men of Galilee, why are you standing there looking at the sky? This Jesus who has been taken up from you into heaven will return in the same way as you have seen him going into heaven."

Responsorial Psalm (Ps 47:2-3, 6-7, 8-9)

R︎. (6) God mounts his throne to shouts of joy: a blare of trumpets for the Lord. *or:* R︎. Alleluia.

All you peoples, clap your hands,
　shout to God with cries of gladness,
for the LORD, the Most High, the awesome,
　is the great king over all the earth.

R︎. God mounts his throne to shouts of joy: a blare of trumpets for the Lord. *or:* R︎. Alleluia.

God mounts his throne amid shouts of joy;
　the LORD, amid trumpet blasts.
Sing praise to God, sing praise;
　sing praise to our king, sing praise.

R︎. God mounts his throne to shouts of joy: a blare of trumpets for the Lord. *or:* R︎. Alleluia.

For king of all the earth is God;
　sing hymns of praise.
God reigns over the nations,
　God sits upon his holy throne.

R︎. God mounts his throne to shouts of joy: a blare of trumpets for the Lord. *or:* R︎. Alleluia.

See Appendix, p. 217, for Second Reading

Reflecting on Living the Gospel

When the disciples see Jesus, "they worshiped, but they doubted." The mixture of postresurrection faith and doubt is not so much skepticism or disbelief as fearful doubt, a struggle to accept the call and its responsibility, knowing only too well their own weakness. We can easily see ourselves, individually and communally, in the same mix of worshiping faith and doubt. True discipleship does not exclude doubt but takes it before God and into the mystery of Christ in whose absent presence we fall down and worship.

Making Connections

The second reading affirms the power of Christ and that the church, his Body, continues his work on earth beyond the ascension. While the gospel has another moment of Jesus's preparing the disciples for his departure, the first reading contains the actual ascension narrative. Here, too, he leaves them with a mission—they are to be his witnesses all through the world. And here, too, there is a promise to return. This is still not the end of the story.

Psalmist Preparation

This psalm, written centuries before the life of Christ, directly connects with the narrative of Jesus ascending into heaven. In Jesus's ascension, God takes his rightful place as ruler over heaven and earth. We respond with rejoicing, even as we await this to be achieved in its fullness. For it remains true that Jesus's kingship is not always clear: sin still happens, suffering still exists, the poor and oppressed become more so. As you prepare this psalm, think of a few ways you wish Jesus's reign were more apparent. Pray for their actualization as you proclaim this psalm; let it be an earnest prayer for the fulfillment of God's promises.

Prayer

All-powerful God,
amidst *shouts of joy* and *a blare of trumpets*
you were lifted into the sky by a cloud,
promising one day to return.
As we who remain set about the mission you gave us,
grant us zeal, persistence, and patience.
Through us, may the whole world
come to know your good news.
Amen.

Gospel (John 17:1-11a; L59A)

Jesus raised his eyes to heaven and said, "Father, the hour has come. Give glory to your son, so that your son may glorify you, just as you gave him authority over all people, so that your son may give eternal life to all you gave him. Now this is eternal life, that they should know you, the only true God, and the one whom you sent, Jesus Christ. I glorified you on earth by accomplishing the work that you gave me to do. Now glorify me, Father, with you, with the glory that I had with you before the world began.

"I revealed your name to those whom you gave me out of the world. They belonged to you, and you gave them to me, and they have kept your word. Now they know that everything you gave me is from you, because the words you gave to me I have given to them, and they accepted them and truly understood that I came from you, and they have believed that you sent me. I pray for them. I do not pray for the world but for the ones you have given me, because they are yours, and everything of mine is yours and everything of yours is mine, and I have been glorified in them. And now I will no longer be in the world, but they are in the world, while I am coming to you."

First Reading (Acts 1:12-14)

After Jesus had been taken up to heaven the apostles returned to Jerusalem from the mount called Olivet, which is near Jerusalem, a sabbath day's journey away.

When they entered the city they went to the upper room where they were staying, Peter and John and James and Andrew, Philip and Thomas, Bartholomew and Matthew, James son of Alphaeus, Simon the Zealot, and Judas son of James. All these devoted themselves with one accord to prayer, together with some women, and Mary the mother of Jesus, and his brothers.

Responsorial Psalm (Ps 27:1, 4, 7-8)

℞. (13) I believe that I shall see the good things of the Lord in the land of the living. *or:* ℞. Alleluia.

The LORD is my light and my salvation;
  whom should I fear?
The LORD is my life's refuge;
  of whom should I be afraid?

℞. I believe that I shall see the good things of the Lord in the land of the living. *or:* ℞. Alleluia.

One thing I ask of the LORD;
  this I seek:
to dwell in the house of the LORD
  all the days of my life,
that I may gaze on the loveliness of the LORD
  and contemplate his temple.

℞. I believe that I shall see the good things of the Lord in the land of the living. *or:* ℞. Alleluia.

Hear, O LORD, the sound of my call;
  have pity on me, and answer me.
Of you my heart speaks; you my glance seeks.

℞. I believe that I shall see the good things of the Lord in the land of the living. *or:* ℞. Alleluia.

See Appendix, p. 217, for Second Reading

Reflecting on Living the Gospel

Fruitful work is done with intention and integrity. As believers who are called to continue God's mission, we will find direction when we are lost and strength when we are weary by keeping our eyes fixed on the ultimate goal. We hear throughout Scripture how Jesus remained connected to the Creator and to his earthly mission through prayer, retreat, and ritual. Let us use this season to pause, seek opportunity for retreat, and grow closer to God through the example of Jesus.

Making Connections

The first reading shows the disciples in the state Jesus describes in the gospel—remaining faithfully in the world after he has returned to heaven. The Holy Spirit has not yet descended, and they have not yet taken up their missions of preaching and service to the poor. Before these things, they devote themselves to prayer, maintaining a relationship with God that will become the basis of their mission in a very short time.

Psalmist Preparation

This psalm affirms Jesus's statement in the gospel that we are all called to share in eternal life. The "land of the living" is not where we are now, where death still has far too great a hold. We are intended for something much greater, something that is beyond the limited imaginings of our small human minds. As you prepare this psalm, spend some time reflecting on your working image of eternal life. How does it compare to this life? What does it look like, sound like, smell like? Who is there with you? Invite God into your imaginings, and bring your image to your proclamation of this week's psalm.

Prayer

God of Sacred Mysteries,
your Son, Jesus, has no hands,
no feet on Earth now but ours.
Fill us with your Spirit, that by our lives
each person you created in love may
see the good things of the Lord in the land of the living.
Help us glorify your name.
Amen.

Gospel **(John 20:19-23; L63A)**

On the evening of that first day of the week, when the doors were locked, where the disciples were, for fear of the Jews, Jesus came and stood in their midst and said to them, "Peace be with you." When he had said this, he showed them his hands and his side. The disciples rejoiced when they saw the Lord. Jesus said to them again, "Peace be with you. As the Father has sent me, so I send you." And when he had said this, he breathed on them and said to them, "Receive the Holy Spirit. Whose sins you forgive are forgiven them, and whose sins you retain are retained."

First Reading **(Acts 2:1-11)**

When the time for Pentecost was fulfilled, they were all in one place together. And suddenly there came from the sky a noise like a strong driving wind, and it filled the entire house in which they were. Then there appeared to them tongues as of fire, which parted and came to rest on each one of them. And they were all filled with the Holy Spirit and began to speak in different tongues, as the Spirit enabled them to proclaim.

Now there were devout Jews from every nation under heaven staying in Jerusalem. At this sound, they gathered in a large crowd, but they were confused because each one heard them speaking in his own language. They were astounded, and in amazement they asked, "Are not all these people who are speaking Galileans? Then how does each of us hear them in his native language? We are Parthians, Medes, and Elamites, inhabitants of Mesopotamia, Judea and Cappadocia, Pontus and Asia, Phrygia and Pamphylia, Egypt and the districts of Libya near Cyrene, as well as travelers from Rome, both Jews and converts to Judaism, Cretans and Arabs, yet we hear them speaking in our own tongues of the mighty acts of God."

Responsorial Psalm (Ps 104:1, 24, 29-30, 31, 34)

R̸. (cf. 30) Lord, send out your Spirit, and renew the face of the earth.
or: R̸. Alleluia.

Bless the LORD, O my soul!
 O LORD, my God, you are great indeed!
How manifold are your works, O LORD!
 The earth is full of your creatures.

R̸. Lord, send out your Spirit, and renew the face of the earth.
or: R̸. Alleluia.

If you take away their breath, they perish
 and return to their dust.
When you send forth your spirit, they are created,
 and you renew the face of the earth.

R̸. Lord, send out your Spirit, and renew the face of the earth.
or: R̸. Alleluia.

May the glory of the LORD endure forever;
 may the LORD be glad in his works!
Pleasing to him be my theme;
 I will be glad in the LORD.

R̸. Lord, send out your Spirit, and renew the face of the earth.
or: R̸. Alleluia.

See Appendix, p. 217, for Second Reading

Reflecting on Living the Gospel

God assures the apostles that even in the depths of their despair, they are not beyond the reach of God's protective, empowering, loving care. Likewise, although fear or hopelessness can make us feel disconnected or isolated from others, we can trust that God will find us wherever we are. We can find solace in the stories of others—honestly and bravely shared in their own unique voices. Perhaps we will even find that our search for God has ended because God is already there—sitting with us in our vulnerability and humanity.

Making Connections

The gospel narrates a small, contained passing of the Holy Spirit. Jesus appears behind locked doors only to those who knew him. He offers them something of a commission, but the story ends the way it started: in a small room in a contained community, behind locked doors. The first reading begins in a similar way but ends with a massively inclusive image: the disciples are preaching not only to those who share their language and culture but to those outside these bounds.

Psalmist Preparation

We have just heard, in the first reading, about God sending out his Spirit, and now in the psalm we ask him to do so again. The Spirit's coming is not a one-and-done deal. Rather, it is an ongoing transmission that brings life. The work of renewing and recreating the earth is never done in our lifetimes. We still wait for Jesus to return and bring it to fullness. As you prepare this psalm, spend some time recognizing ways the Holy Spirit is active in your life. Also acknowledge where you might need the Spirit, and ask God to pour it forth into your individual life as well as the life of the church.

Prayer

Triune God,
the fullness of your presence
is made manifest in the activity of your Holy Spirit,
enlivening, refreshing, propelling, and quickening.
Creator God, Redeeming Son:
send out your Spirit, and renew the face of the earth.
Set us ablaze with your love, gift us with your holy presence.
Amen.

Gospel (John 3:16-18; L164A)

God so loved the world that he gave his only Son, so that everyone who believes in him might not perish but might have eternal life. For God did not send his Son into the world to condemn the world, but that the world might be saved through him. Whoever believes in him will not be condemned, but whoever does not believe has already been condemned, because he has not believed in the name of the only Son of God.

First Reading (Exod 34:4b-6, 8-9)

Early in the morning Moses went up Mount Sinai as the LORD had commanded him, taking along the two stone tablets.

Having come down in a cloud, the LORD stood with Moses there and proclaimed his name, "LORD." Thus the LORD passed before him and cried out, "The LORD, the LORD, a merciful and gracious God, slow to anger and rich in kindness and fidelity." Moses at once bowed down to the ground in worship. Then he said, "If I find favor with you, O LORD, do come along in our company. This is indeed a stiff-necked people; yet pardon our wickedness and sins, and receive us as your own."

Responsorial Psalm (Dan 3:52, 53, 54, 55)

R̖. (52b) Glory and praise for ever!

Blessed are you, O Lord, the God of our fathers,
    praiseworthy and exalted above all forever;
and blessed is your holy and glorious name,
    praiseworthy and exalted above all for all ages.

R̖. Glory and praise for ever!

Blessed are you in the temple of your holy glory,
    praiseworthy and glorious above all forever.

R̖. Glory and praise for ever!

Blessed are you on the throne of your kingdom,
    praiseworthy and exalted above all forever.

R̖. Glory and praise for ever!

Blessed are you who look into the depths
    from your throne upon the cherubim,
    praiseworthy and exalted above all forever.

℟. Glory and praise for ever!

See Appendix, p. 217, for Second Reading

Reflecting on Living the Gospel

The mystery of God that all three readings proclaim is love—and love is never solitary, never static or finished. Theology has tried to express this idea in the word *perichorésis* or "dance/choreography."

Choreography suggests dynamic, mobile partnership: encircling, encompassing, permeating, enveloping, outstretching. As theologian Catherine Mowry LaCugna writes: "There are neither leaders nor followers in the divine dance, only an eternal movement of reciprocal giving and receiving, giving again and receiving again. . . . The image of the dance forbids us to think of God as solitary."

Making Connections

The second reading finally names all three members of the Trinity explicitly on this Trinity Sunday. St. Paul uses their names as a greeting, one we still use at Mass today. This is a powerful greeting. We begin everything we do in the names of these three persons in one God. The familiarity of this triad—Father, Son, and Spirit—can make us forget that there is a beautiful mystery at play here. God's very essence is relationship, is love, to the point that God needs to be three persons so that the love has someplace to go.

Psalmist Preparation

Sometimes psalms of praise are repetitive in nature, and it can be tempting to think of them as boring. But this form of Hebrew poetry has an elegance to it; the repeated phrase "praiseworthy and exalted above all forever" cycles back after lines that draw us deeper and deeper into something that cannot actually be expressed in words. This is a lovely, poetic depiction of the mystery of the Trinity that we celebrate today. We cannot fully comprehend it, but we can be drawn more fully into it. As our understanding grows deeper and realer, so too can our praise.

Prayer

God,
you are a holy community, lover, beloved, and loving.
Formed in your image, we too are called
to be with one another in a holy community of love.
Your love saves us, brings us peace and justice,
and leads us to eternal life.
Glory and praise forever!
Amen.

Gospel (John 6:51-58; L167A)

Jesus said to the Jewish crowds: "I am the living bread that came down from heaven; whoever eats this bread will live forever; and the bread that I will give is my flesh for the life of the world."

The Jews quarreled among themselves, saying, "How can this man give us his flesh to eat?" Jesus said to them, "Amen, amen, I say to you, unless you eat the flesh of the Son of Man and drink his blood, you do not have life within you. Whoever eats my flesh and drinks my blood has eternal life, and I will raise him on the last day. For my flesh is true food, and my blood is true drink. Whoever eats my flesh and drinks my blood remains in me and I in him. Just as the living Father sent me and I have life because of the Father, so also the one who feeds on me will have life because of me. This is the bread that came down from heaven. Unlike your ancestors who ate and still died, whoever eats this bread will live forever."

First Reading (Deut 8:2-3, 14b-16a)

Moses said to the people: "Remember how for forty years now the LORD, your God, has directed all your journeying in the desert, so as to test you by affliction and find out whether or not it was your intention to keep his commandments. He therefore let you be afflicted with hunger, and then fed you with manna, a food unknown to you and your fathers, in order to show you that not by bread alone does one live, but by every word that comes forth from the mouth of the LORD.

"Do not forget the LORD, your God, who brought you out of the land of Egypt, that place of slavery; who guided you through the vast and terrible desert with its saraph serpents and scorpions, its parched and waterless ground; who brought forth water for you from the flinty rock and fed you in the desert with manna, a food unknown to your fathers."

Responsorial Psalm (Ps 147:12-13, 14-15, 19-20)

R̖. (12) Praise the Lord, Jerusalem. *or:* R̖. Alleluia.

Glorify the LORD, O Jerusalem;
  praise your God, O Zion.
For he has strengthened the bars of your gates;
  he has blessed your children within you.

R̖. Praise the Lord, Jerusalem. *or:* R̖. Alleluia.

He has granted peace in your borders;
  with the best of wheat he fills you.
He sends forth his command to the earth;
  swiftly runs his word!

R̖. Praise the Lord, Jerusalem. *or:* R̖. Alleluia.

He has proclaimed his word to Jacob,
  his statutes and his ordinances to Israel.
He has not done thus for any other nation;
  his ordinances he has not made known to them. Alleluia.

R̖. Praise the Lord, Jerusalem. *or:* R̖. Alleluia.

See Appendix, p. 217, for Second Reading

Reflecting on Living the Gospel

This is the day we acknowledge that we have Christ in our blood, that we are the people who are hungry and thirsty for God. It recalls Holy Thursday, the first day of the Triduum, and the God who feeds us with the real eucharistic presence of Jesus. On the Sunday after we have celebrated the mystery of the Most Holy Trinity and the communion between the Father, the Son, and the Holy Spirit, we remember that we enter most intimately into this communion in the Eucharist.

Making Connections

The first reading shows that God has a long history of providing food and drink for God's people. The Eucharist carries on this long tradition, but in an entirely new way that gives life previously unimaginable. The second reading reminds us that the Eucharist is a way of participating in the life of Jesus himself. We become his Body by participating. We are also bound together, becoming united in a reality that transcends all the human divisions we continue to enforce.

Psalmist Preparation

Here we offer praise for the special gift with which God has entrusted God's people. As you prepare this psalm, reflect on eucharistic experiences from your own lifetime. Do any jump out as particularly powerful experiences of God's presence? How has the reception of Communion and the regular discipline of liturgical participation shaped your faith? When you proclaim this psalm, let its praise be for all that the Eucharist has been to you—and all that will still unfold in your ongoing relationship with Jesus there.

Prayer

Sustaining Presence,
you created us to be your people,
to be your holy city, Jerusalem, now and always.
Preserve us with your body and teach us with your word.
Let us *[p]raise the Lord*, we who call ourselves Christians,
and forever lift up our hearts to his holy name.
Amen.

Gospel (Matt 9:36–10:8; L91A)

At the sight of the crowds, Jesus' heart was moved with pity for them because they were troubled and abandoned, like sheep without a shepherd. Then he said to his disciples, "The harvest is abundant but the laborers are few; so ask the master of the harvest to send out laborers for his harvest." Then he summoned his twelve disciples and gave them authority over unclean spirits to drive them out and to cure every disease and every illness.

The names of the twelve apostles are these: first, Simon called Peter, and his brother Andrew; James, the son of Zebedee, and his brother John; Philip and Bartholomew, Thomas and Matthew the tax collector; James, the son of Alphaeus, and Thaddeus; Simon from Cana, and Judas Iscariot who betrayed him.

Jesus sent out these twelve after instructing them thus, "Do not go into pagan territory or enter a Samaritan town. Go rather to the lost sheep of the house of Israel. As you go, make this proclamation: 'The kingdom of heaven is at hand.' Cure the sick, raise the dead, cleanse lepers, drive out demons. Without cost you have received; without cost you are to give."

First Reading (Exod 19:2-6a)

In those days, the Israelites came to the desert of Sinai and pitched camp. While Israel was encamped here in front of the mountain, Moses went up the mountain to God. Then the Lord called to him and said, "Thus shall you say to the house of Jacob; tell the Israelites: You have seen for yourselves how I treated the Egyptians and how I bore you up on eagle wings and brought you here to myself. Therefore, if you hearken to my voice and keep my covenant, you shall be my special possession, dearer to me than all other people, though all the earth is mine. You shall be to me a kingdom of priests, a holy nation."

Responsorial Psalm (Ps 100:1-2, 3, 5)

℟. (3c) We are his people: the sheep of his flock.

Sing joyfully to the LORD, all you lands;
    serve the LORD with gladness;
    come before him with joyful song.

℟. We are his people: the sheep of his flock.

Know that the LORD is God;
    he made us, his we are;
    his people, the flock he tends.

℟. We are his people: the sheep of his flock.

The LORD is good:
    his kindness endures forever,
    and his faithfulness to all generations.

℟. We are his people: the sheep of his flock.

Second Reading (Rom 5:6-11)

Reflecting on Living the Gospel

The passage of Matthew's gospel that we hear today includes the only occasion that Matthew uses the word *apostle*, meaning "sent one," to describe the follower of Jesus. Whereas the meaning of *disciple* is "learner," here the emphasis is on their being *sent out*. If fishermen (two sets of brothers, with the family dynamics that might involve), a tax collector, a hot-headed revolutionary Zealot, a traitor, and the rest, could be chosen by Jesus as the first sent ones, then surely there is hope for the church today.

Making Connections

The first reading affirms Jesus's understanding of Israel as God's particularly beloved people. They are to be "a kingdom of priests," tasked with acting as something of a liaison between God and the rest of the world. In the gospel, the disciples take part in this priesthood in a new way, sent out to bring God back to Israel and Israel back to God. Ultimately, they will be further commissioned to go to all nations; the Holy Spirit at Pentecost will enable them to speak beyond the boundaries of their own language and culture.

Psalmist Preparation

This psalm expands the first reading's notion of Israel as God's chosen people; we, too, have been adopted by God in baptism and now belong to this beloved assembly. This psalm is appropriate for the image of a flock. It has a simple joy to it that suggests the childlike faith with which we are called to follow our shepherd. As you prepare this psalm, think of moments when your faith was simple and easy, when God's presence was clear and your response of love came naturally. Give thanks to God for these moments, which often help sustain us when faith feels more complicated and God's presence is harder to discern. Know that God remains with you; that promise is clear.

Prayer

God of Peace, God of Rest,
your son is for us a loving shepherd,
safety and security through the night.
We are his people: the sheep of his flock.
We praise you for your kindness and faithfulness.
Grant us always your reconciliation and salvation.
Amen.

JUNE 25, 2023

Gospel (Matt 10:26-33; L94A)

Jesus said to the Twelve: "Fear no one. Nothing is concealed that will not be revealed, nor secret that will not be known. What I say to you in the darkness, speak in the light; what you hear whispered, proclaim on the housetops. And do not be afraid of those who kill the body but cannot kill the soul; rather, be afraid of the one who can destroy both soul and body in Gehenna. Are not two sparrows sold for a small coin? Yet not one of them falls to the ground without your Father's knowledge. Even all the hairs of your head are counted. So do not be afraid; you are worth more than many sparrows. Everyone who acknowledges me before others I will acknowledge before my heavenly Father. But whoever denies me before others, I will deny before my heavenly Father."

First Reading (Jer 20:10-13)

Jeremiah said:

"I hear the whisperings of many:
  'Terror on every side!
  Denounce! Let us denounce him!'
All those who were my friends
  are on the watch for any misstep of mine.
'Perhaps he will be trapped; then we can prevail,
  and take our vengeance on him.'
But the LORD is with me, like a mighty champion:
  my persecutors will stumble, they will not triumph.
In their failure they will be put to utter shame,
  to lasting, unforgettable confusion.
O LORD of hosts, you who test the just,
  who probe mind and heart,
let me witness the vengeance you take on them,
  for to you I have entrusted my cause.

Sing to the LORD,
  praise the LORD,
for he has rescued the life of the poor
  from the power of the wicked!"

Responsorial Psalm (Ps 69:8-10, 14, 17, 33-35)

℟. (14c) Lord, in your great love, answer me.

For your sake I bear insult,
  and shame covers my face.
I have become an outcast to my brothers,
  a stranger to my children,
because zeal for your house consumes me,
  and the insults of those who blaspheme you fall upon me.

℟. Lord, in your great love, answer me.

I pray to you, O LORD,
  for the time of your favor, O God!
In your great kindness answer me
  with your constant help.
Answer me, O LORD, for bounteous is your kindness;
  in your great mercy turn toward me.

℟. Lord, in your great love, answer me.

"See, you lowly ones, and be glad;
  you who seek God, may your hearts revive!
For the LORD hears the poor,
  and his own who are in bonds he spurns not.
Let the heavens and the earth praise him,
  the seas and whatever moves in them!"

℟. Lord, in your great love, answer me.

Second Reading (Rom 5:12-15)

Reflecting on Living the Gospel

What are the difficulties in climbing to the contemporary "housetops" where the right words can be spoken and heard? Married people struggling with fidelity, young people at war with their hormones, those with disabilities longing to be recognized first of all as people, men and women searching for their sexual identity, the poor and disadvantaged who are ashamed or angry: all of these need Christians to first of all listen to and then respond to their stories.

Making Connections

Jeremiah here acknowledges the same fear the disciples experience in the gospel. Being a messenger for God can make us unpopular; encountering God often calls people to change in ways for which they are not ready, and their resulting scorn is sometimes directed at those who bring the message. But again, strength is found in God's companionship and protection. Courage is called for, and it is justified, because the one who goes with us can do all things.

Psalmist Preparation

The psalm echoes the sentiments of both the gospel and the first reading: a life of faith is not always easy. Sometimes, in the context of a sinful world, it even causes suffering. There is reason for fear. But there is also reason for courage, for we do not face our suffering alone. God, who is all-powerful, promises to accompany us always in love. As you prepare this psalm, reflect on any fears you have about living your faith. Where do you need an increase in courage? Know that God hears and answers the plea you make in this psalm.

Prayer

God of the Prophets,
at times, speaking your truth and living your love
brings only insults and loneliness,
and seems a failure in the world's eyes.
Hear my call, hear my cry: *in your great love, answer me.*
The life of a Christian is difficult, but full of hope:
give us joy in your presence.
Amen.

Gospel (Matt 10:37-42; L97A)

Jesus said to his apostles: "Whoever loves father or mother more than me is not worthy of me, and whoever loves son or daughter more than me is not worthy of me; and whoever does not take up his cross and follow after me is not worthy of me. Whoever finds his life will lose it, and whoever loses his life for my sake will find it. Whoever receives you receives me, and whoever receives me receives the one who sent me. Whoever receives a prophet because he is a prophet will receive a prophet's reward, and whoever receives a righteous man because he is a righteous man will receive a righteous man's reward. And whoever gives only a cup of cold water to one of these little ones to drink because the little one is a disciple—amen, I say to you, he will surely not lose his reward."

First Reading (2 Kgs 4:8-11, 14-16a)

One day Elisha came to Shunem, where there was a woman of influence, who urged him to dine with her. Afterward, whenever he passed by, he used to stop there to dine. So she said to her husband, "I know that Elisha is a holy man of God. Since he visits us often, let us arrange a little room on the roof and furnish it for him with a bed, table, chair, and lamp, so that when he comes to us he can stay there." Sometime later Elisha arrived and stayed in the room overnight.

Later Elisha asked, "Can something be done for her?" His servant Gehazi answered, "Yes! She has no son, and her husband is getting on in years." Elisha said, "Call her." When the woman had been called and stood at the door, Elisha promised, "This time next year you will be fondling a baby son."

Responsorial Psalm **(Ps 89:2-3, 16-17, 18-19)**

℟. (2a) For ever I will sing the goodness of the Lord.

The promises of the LORD I will sing forever,
  through all generations my mouth shall proclaim your faithfulness.
For you have said, "My kindness is established forever";
  in heaven you have confirmed your faithfulness.

℟. For ever I will sing the goodness of the Lord.

Blessed the people who know the joyful shout;
  in the light of your countenance, O LORD, they walk.
At your name they rejoice all the day,
  and through your justice they are exalted.

℟. For ever I will sing the goodness of the Lord.

You are the splendor of their strength,
  and by your favor our horn is exalted.
For to the LORD belongs our shield,
  and to the Holy One of Israel, our king.

℟. For ever I will sing the goodness of the Lord.

Second Reading **(Rom 6:3-4, 8-11)**

Reflecting on Living the Gospel

Today, the simple statement, "I am a Christian," can still bring martyr-
dom in some places. Though that's not the case here in the United States,
no committed Christian can escape the demanding priorities of the cross
that Jesus describes in today's gospel reading. We do not pray for the
cross, but we accept its often surprising arrival, trying to recognize it for
what it is: a challenge to trust in God and God's future, and to discover
that self-giving is self-fulfillment.

Making Connections

The first reading shows a practice of radical hospitality, the same kind
to which we are called by the gospel. The Shunammite woman and her
husband do not just provide for Elisha's needs as is convenient for them.
They rearrange their very lives and home to make space for him. In the
end, this is what hospitality is all about—making space for others, in our
homes, in our lives, and in our hearts.

Psalmist Preparation

This is a lovely psalm to proclaim; you get to sing about singing and to pledge through your very song the church's intention to always offer praise for God's goodness. The vow we make here is a big one: "forever" is a lot to promise! But we can make it precisely because of the goodness of the Lord. It is God's faithfulness that comes first, and because God fulfills his promises, we can fulfill ours. As you prepare this psalm, seek out evidence of God's goodness in your own life. Sing this psalm in thanksgiving for what you find and let it be an earnest prayer of praise.

Prayer

Good and Gracious God,
you fulfill your promises to your people,
giving new life to those who live your covenant.
Forever let us *sing the goodness of the Lord.*
You are holy, our strength, our deliverer.
Bring us to more deeply live your truth
and to follow in your ways.
Amen.

Gospel (Matt 11:25-30; L100A)

At that time Jesus exclaimed: "I give praise to you, Father, Lord of heaven and earth, for although you have hidden these things from the wise and the learned you have revealed them to little ones. Yes, Father, such has been your gracious will. All things have been handed over to me by my Father. No one knows the Son except the Father, and no one knows the Father except the Son and anyone to whom the Son wishes to reveal him.

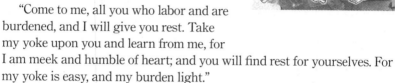

"Come to me, all you who labor and are burdened, and I will give you rest. Take my yoke upon you and learn from me, for I am meek and humble of heart; and you will find rest for yourselves. For my yoke is easy, and my burden light."

First Reading (Zech 9:9-10)

Thus says the LORD:
Rejoice heartily, O daughter Zion,
    shout for joy, O daughter Jerusalem!
See, your king shall come to you;
    a just savior is he,
meek, and riding on an ass,
    on a colt, the foal of an ass.
He shall banish the chariot from Ephraim,
    and the horse from Jerusalem;
the warrior's bow shall be banished,
    and he shall proclaim peace to the nations.
His dominion shall be from sea to sea,
    and from the River to the ends of the earth.

Responsorial Psalm (Ps 145:1-2, 8-9, 10-11, 13-14)

℟. (cf. 1) I will praise your name for ever, my king and my God.
or: ℟. Alleluia.

I will extol you, O my God and King,
 and I will bless your name forever and ever.
Every day will I bless you,
 and I will praise your name forever and ever.

℟. I will praise your name for ever, my king and my God. *or:* ℟. Alleluia.

The LORD is gracious and merciful,
 slow to anger and of great kindness.
The LORD is good to all
 and compassionate toward all his works.

℟. I will praise your name for ever, my king and my God. *or:* ℟. Alleluia.

Let all your works give you thanks, O LORD,
 and let your faithful ones bless you.
Let them discourse of the glory of your kingdom
 and speak of your might.

℟. I will praise your name for ever, my king and my God. *or:* ℟. Alleluia.

The LORD is faithful in all his words
 and holy in all his works.
The LORD lifts up all who are falling
 and raises up all who are bowed down.

℟. I will praise your name for ever, my king and my God. *or:* ℟. Alleluia.

Second Reading (Rom 8:9, 11-13)

Reflecting on Living the Gospel

In the gospel reading we hear today, Matthew gives us one of our very
few glimpses into the prayer of Jesus. As when he had earlier taught his
disciples to pray, Jesus addresses God as "Father," not to idolize a name or
gender or metaphor, but to focus on *a relationship*: the reign of his Abba
over his life and the lives of all those who become daughters and sons of
this same God by accepting Jesus as the Word and Wisdom of God.

Making Connections

The first reading also speaks a word of consolation: God comes to save
us, and our response is to rejoice. God is not a God of war who will deal
harsh justice to our enemies. Rather, he comes meekly, in a way we

would not expect. He banishes not Israel's enemies but the very tools of war. Once again, God subverts our expectations. He does not engage in the futile means humans have for fighting each other but rather bypasses the fight altogether.

Psalmist Preparation

This is an iconic psalm of praise, pouring out thanksgiving for all God has done and continues to do for us. Our response is one of gratitude and of speaking. When we experience the fullness of God's love we are compelled to share what we have seen with others. This psalm is also a familiar one—one of the frequent flyers of Ordinary Time. As you prepare to proclaim it this week, consider ways you have witnessed God at work in your own life. If time permits, write your own psalm of praise and use your own words to express your gratitude for all God has done. Bring the energy and love of your new psalm into your proclamation of these old words.

Prayer

Savior and Solace,
with you is justice and peace, rest and respite.
We shall *praise your name forever*
for you call us to childlike faith,
to abandon riches, power, and influence.
Rather, your reign is one of dependence on you,
revealed in your son, Jesus Christ,
who is Lord for ever and ever.
Amen.

Gospel (Matt 13:1-23 [or Matt 13:1-9]; L103A)

On that day, Jesus went out of the house and sat down by the sea. Such large crowds gathered around him that he got into a boat and sat down, and the whole crowd stood along the shore. And he spoke to them at length in parables, saying: "A sower went out to sow. And as he sowed, some seed fell on the path, and birds came and ate it up. Some fell on rocky ground, where it had little soil. It sprang up at once because the soil was not deep, and when the sun rose it was scorched, and it withered for lack of roots. Some seed fell among thorns, and the thorns grew up and choked it. But some seed fell on rich soil, and produced fruit, a hundred or sixty or thirtyfold. Whoever has ears ought to hear."

The disciples approached him and said, "Why do you speak to them in parables?" He said to them in reply, "Because knowledge of the mysteries of the kingdom of heaven has been granted to you, but to them it has not been granted. To anyone who has, more will be given and he will grow rich; from anyone who has not, even what he has will be taken away. This is why I speak to them in parables, because

they look but do not see and hear but do not listen or understand.
Isaiah's prophecy is fulfilled in them, which says:
You shall indeed hear but not understand,
    you shall indeed look but never see.
Gross is the heart of this people,
    they will hardly hear with their ears,
    they have closed their eyes,
    lest they see with their eyes
    and hear with their ears
and understand with their hearts and be converted,
    and I heal them.

"But blessed are your eyes, because they see, and your ears, because they hear. Amen, I say to you, many prophets and righteous people longed to see what you see but did not see it, and to hear what you hear but did not hear it.

"Hear then the parable of the sower. The seed sown on the path is the one who hears the word of the kingdom without understanding it, and the evil one comes and steals away what was sown in his heart. The seed sown on rocky ground is the one who hears the word and receives it at once with joy. But he has no root and lasts only for a time. When some tribulation or persecution comes because of the word, he immediately falls away. The seed sown among thorns is the one who hears the word, but then worldly anxiety and the lure of riches choke the word and it bears no fruit. But the seed sown on rich soil is the one who hears the word and understands it, who indeed bears fruit and yields a hundred or sixty or thirtyfold."

First Reading (Isa 55:10-11)

Thus says the Lord:
Just as from the heavens
　　the rain and snow come down
and do not return there
　　till they have watered the earth,
　　making it fertile and fruitful,
giving seed to the one who sows
　　and bread to the one who eats,
so shall my word be
　　that goes forth from my mouth;
my word shall not return to me void,
　　but shall do my will,
　　achieving the end for which I sent it.

Responsorial Psalm (Ps 65:10, 11, 12-13, 14)

R̥. (Luke 8:8) The seed that falls on good ground will yield a fruitful harvest.

You have visited the land and watered it;
　　greatly have you enriched it.
God's watercourses are filled;
　　you have prepared the grain.

R̥. The seed that falls on good ground will yield a fruitful harvest.

Thus have you prepared the land: drenching its furrows,
   breaking up its clods,
softening it with showers,
   blessing its yield.

R♭. The seed that falls on good ground will yield a fruitful harvest.

You have crowned the year with your bounty,
   and your paths overflow with a rich harvest;
the untilled meadows overflow with it,
   and rejoicing clothes the hills.

R♭. The seed that falls on good ground will yield a fruitful harvest.

The fields are garmented with flocks
   and the valleys blanketed with grain.
   They shout and sing for joy.

R♭. The seed that falls on good ground will yield a fruitful harvest.

Second Reading (Rom 8:18-23)

Reflecting on Living the Gospel

The seed is a wonderful symbol of the kingdom. Small, hard, unattractive to the senses, yet holding within the hope of growth, of harvest, of life. It remains only a seed, unless it surrenders itself to an environment that can realize its potential. When that happens, the seed grows gently, quietly; there is no instant produce. This is a good parable for Ordinary Time, with the festal seasons behind and before us and the word of God, planted within us, germinating slowly in the soil of our daily lives.

Making Connections

The first reading and psalm echo the farming imagery of the gospel. God's word is likened to the rain that comes forth from heaven to nourish the earth and to feed us. The second reading pairs our seed and fruit imagery with another of nature's great wonders—that of childbirth. Labor pains are another reflection of God's cyclical work, for great pain and groaning bring new life and abundant joy. The pain of labor, like the suffering of Christ, is life-giving. It is not pain without purpose.

Psalmist Preparation

This is a gorgeous, underused psalm. It praises God for the beauty of the earth and the wisdom with which God designed its seasons to feed and nourish us. If you can, sit outside as you rehearse this psalm. Use all your senses to notice the lush growth and vibrant life of summertime: see greenery, hear birdsong, and so on. Notice how your singing voice sounds outside; open air often carries sound differently from closed spaces. Notice all that God has created and give thanks for it; bring your gratitude for your little corner of the natural world into your proclamation of this psalm.

Prayer
Creator God,
you call us into the mission field,
to plant, tend, and reap.
The seed that falls on good ground
will yield a fruitful harvest.
Help us find open ears and willing hearts,
that all may come to know and help create
your reign of wholeness and love.
Amen.

Gospel (Matt 13:24-43
[or Matt 13:24-30]; L106A)

Jesus proposed another parable to the crowds, saying: "The kingdom of heaven may be likened to a man who sowed good seed in his field. While everyone was asleep his enemy came and sowed weeds all through the wheat, and then went off. When the crop grew and bore fruit, the weeds appeared as well. The slaves of the householder came to him and said, 'Master, did you not sow good seed in your field? Where have the weeds come from?' He answered, 'An enemy has done this.' His slaves said to him, 'Do you want us to go and pull them up?' He replied, 'No, if you pull up the weeds you might uproot the wheat along with them. Let them grow together until harvest; then at harvest time I will say to the harvesters, "First collect the weeds and tie them in bundles for burning; but gather the wheat into my barn."'"

He proposed another parable to them. "The kingdom of heaven is like a mustard seed that a person took and sowed in a field. It is the smallest of all the seeds, yet when full-grown it is the largest of plants. It becomes a large bush, and the 'birds of the sky come and dwell in its branches.'"

He spoke to them another parable. "The kingdom of heaven is like yeast that a woman took and mixed with three measures of wheat flour until the whole batch was leavened."

All these things Jesus spoke to the crowds in parables. He spoke to them only in parables, to fulfill what had been said through the prophet:

I will open my mouth in parables,
I will announce what has lain hidden from the foundation of the world.

Then, dismissing the crowds, he went into the house. His disciples approached him and said, "Explain to us the parable of the weeds in the field." He said in reply, "He who sows good seed is the Son of Man, the field is the world, the good seed the children of the kingdom. The weeds are the children of the evil one, and the enemy who sows them is the devil. The harvest is the end of the age, and the harvesters are angels. Just as weeds are collected and burned up with fire, so will it be at the end of the age. The Son of Man will send his angels, and they will collect out of his kingdom all who cause others to sin and all evildoers. They will throw them into the fiery furnace, where there will be wailing and grinding of teeth. Then the righteous will shine like the sun in the kingdom of their Father. Whoever has ears ought to hear."

First Reading (Wis 12:13, 16-19)

There is no god besides you who have the care of all,
  that you need show you have not unjustly condemned.
For your might is the source of justice;
  your mastery over all things makes you lenient to all.
For you show your might when the perfection of your power is
    disbelieved;
  and in those who know you, you rebuke temerity.
But though you are master of might, you judge with clemency,
  and with much lenience you govern us;
  for power, whenever you will, attends you.
And you taught your people, by these deeds,
  that those who are just must be kind;
and you gave your children good ground for hope
  that you would permit repentance for their sins.

Responsorial Psalm (Ps 86:5-6, 9-10, 15-16)

℟. (5a) Lord, you are good and forgiving.

You, O LORD, are good and forgiving,
  abounding in kindness to all who call upon you.
Hearken, O LORD, to my prayer
  and attend to the sound of my pleading.

℟. Lord, you are good and forgiving.

All the nations you have made shall come
  and worship you, O LORD,
  and glorify your name.
For you are great, and you do wondrous deeds;
  you alone are God.

℟. Lord, you are good and forgiving.

You, O LORD, are a God merciful and gracious,
  slow to anger, abounding in kindness and fidelity.
Turn toward me, and have pity on me;
  give your strength to your servant.

℟. Lord, you are good and forgiving.

Second Reading (Rom 8:26-27)

Reflecting on Living the Gospel

In the short parable of the mustard seed there is encouragement for the Christian community struggling with its small beginnings or, like today's church, faced in some places with the diminution of what once was "big," such as priestly and religious vocations or well-attended Masses. God's kingdom is not imaged as a towering, majestic cedar that Ezekiel describes (see Ezek 17:3-10). For the reign of the kingdom, says Jesus, small seeds are enough to grow into welcoming bushes where people can rest and nest.

Making Connections

The gospel shows God as a farmer who rather harshly separates the intended harvest from the weeds that are not meant to be there. The first reading balances this image by reminding us that this is a God of forgiveness, known for leniency and repeated mercies. The psalm echoes this theme, praising God for the abounding kindness and never-ending patience that none of us deserves but which we receive anyway.

Psalmist Preparation

This psalm praises God for the endless forgiveness that characterizes God's dealings with us. None of us really deserves the grace God pours forth abundantly, but God gives it anyway. If you can, participate in the sacrament of reconciliation this week as part of your preparation of this psalm. This is a private sacrament, but it has a communal dimension as well; it is as an assembly that we receive God's mercy. Let your experience of God's mercy illuminate these words as you lead the assembly in praise for God's mercy for all of us.

Prayer

Reconciling God,
your son took our sins to the cross
that all may be created anew, one in you and your iove.
Lord, you are good and forgiving.
May we too forgive as you do, love as you do,
and one day bring all to fulfillment
in your merciful presence.
Amen.

Gospel (Matt 13:44-52 [or Matt 13:44-46]; L109A)

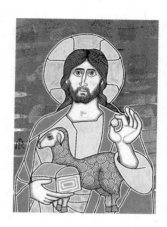

Jesus said to his disciples: "The kingdom of heaven is like a treasure buried in a field, which a person finds and hides again, and out of joy goes and sells all that he has and buys that field. Again, the kingdom of heaven is like a merchant searching for fine pearls. When he finds a pearl of great price, he goes and sells all that he has and buys it. Again, the kingdom of heaven is like a net thrown into the sea, which collects fish of every kind. When it is full they haul it ashore and sit down to put what is good into buckets. What is bad they throw away. Thus it will be at the end of the age. The angels will go out and separate the wicked from the righteous and throw them into the fiery furnace, where there will be wailing and grinding of teeth.

"Do you understand all these things?" They answered, "Yes." And he replied, "Then every scribe who has been instructed in the kingdom of heaven is like the head of a household who brings from his storeroom both the new and the old."

First Reading (1 Kgs 3:5, 7-12)

The Lord appeared to Solomon in a dream at night. God said, "Ask something of me and I will give it to you." Solomon answered: "O Lord, my God, you have made me, your servant, king to succeed my father David; but I am a mere youth, not knowing at all how to act. I serve you in the midst of the people whom you have chosen, a people so vast that it cannot be numbered or counted. Give your servant, therefore, an understanding heart to judge your people and to distinguish right from wrong. For who is able to govern this vast people of yours?"

The Lord was pleased that Solomon made this request. So God said to him: "Because you have asked for this— not for a long life for yourself, nor for riches, nor for the life of your enemies, but for understanding so that you may know what is right— I do as you requested. I give you a heart so wise and understanding that there has never been anyone like you up to now, and after you there will come no one to equal you."

Responsorial Psalm (Ps 119:57, 72, 76-77, 127-128, 129-130)

℟. (97a) Lord, I love your commands.

I have said, O Lord, that my part
  is to keep your words.
The law of your mouth is to me more precious
  than thousands of gold and silver pieces.

℟. Lord, I love your commands.

Let your kindness comfort me
  according to your promise to your servants.
Let your compassion come to me that I may live,
  for your law is my delight.

℟. Lord, I love your commands.

For I love your commands
  more than gold, however fine.
For in all your precepts I go forward;
  every false way I hate.

℟. Lord, I love your commands.

Wonderful are your decrees;
  therefore I observe them.
The revelation of your words sheds light,
  giving understanding to the simple.

℟. Lord, I love your commands.

Second Reading (Rom 8:28-30)

Reflecting on Living the Gospel

A dragnet was a large net supported by floats and used for surface fishing. Its catch was indiscriminate: edible and inedible, ritually clean and unclean, marketable or worthless, the fish would be sorted out by the fishermen when brought ashore. The dragnet catch is an image of the Christian community of committed disciples and sinners, of good and evil—the mix that we can recognize in ourselves. There will, however, come a moment of end-time judgment when disciples will be finally accountable.

Making Connections

Solomon asks for something that pleases God: an understanding heart. He pursues wisdom with the wholeheartedness with which we are to pursue the kingdom, which tells us something else about what pursuing the kingdom entails. It is deeply related to this wisdom. The psalm continues this theme, for encountering God's leadership—even his commands—inspires a response of love from us.

Psalmist Preparation

This psalm praises God's commands, God's law, as a great gift or treasure. The psalmist's response to it is not one of begrudging compliance but of grateful joy. The law is seen as a gift that God has given in order that we might participate in God's kingdom and share in God's eternal life. As you prepare this psalm, think about how you respond to the idea of God as a king who rules and leads. As you understand God right now, is this someone you want to follow? Does the idea of obedience to God bring you joy or does it feel like a burden?

Prayer

Divine Wisdom,
your ways are not our ways,
yet those with understanding hearts,
who earnestly seek you and *love your commands*
find joy and hope in you.
Help us always to treasure our relationship with you,
and to pursue an ever-deeper love of you, with you,
and with all you have created.
Amen.

Gospel (Matt 17:1-9; L614)

Jesus took Peter, James, and his brother, John, and led them up a high mountain by themselves. And he was transfigured before them; his face shone like the sun and his clothes became white as light. And behold, Moses and Elijah appeared to them, conversing with him. Then Peter said to Jesus in reply, "Lord, it is good that we are here. If you wish, I will make three tents here, one for you, one for Moses, and one for Elijah." While he was still speaking, behold, a bright cloud cast a shadow over them, then from the cloud came a voice  that said, "This is my beloved Son, with whom I am well pleased; listen to him." When the disciples heard this, they fell prostrate and were very much afraid. But Jesus came and touched them, saying, "Rise, and do not be afraid." And when the disciples raised their eyes, they saw no one else but Jesus alone.

As they were coming down from the mountain, Jesus charged them, "Do not tell the vision to anyone until the Son of Man has been raised from the dead."

First Reading (Dan 7:9-10, 13-14)

As I watched:
> Thrones were set up
>> and the Ancient One took his throne.
> His clothing was snow bright,
>> and the hair on his head as white as wool;
> his throne was flames of fire,
>> with wheels of burning fire.
> A surging stream of fire
>> flowed out from where he sat;
> thousands upon thousands were ministering to him,
>> and myriads upon myriads attended him.

The court was convened and the books were opened.

As the visions during the night continued, I saw
> one like a Son of man coming,
>> on the clouds of heaven;

when he reached the Ancient One
and was presented before him,
the one like a Son of man received dominion, glory, and kingship;
all peoples, nations, and languages serve him.
His dominion is an everlasting dominion
that shall not be taken away,
his kingship shall not be destroyed.

Responsorial Psalm (Ps 97:1-2, 5-6, 9)

℞. (1a, 9a) The Lord is king, the Most High over all the earth.

The LORD is king; let the earth rejoice;
let the many islands be glad.
Clouds and darkness are round about him;
justice and judgment are the foundation of his throne.

℞. The Lord is king, the Most High over all the earth.

The mountains melt like wax before the LORD,
before the LORD of all the earth.
The heavens proclaim his justice;
all peoples see his glory.

℞. The Lord is king, the Most High over all the earth.

Because you, O LORD, are the Most High over all the earth,
exalted far above all gods.

℞. The Lord is king, the Most High over all the earth.

See Appendix, p. 218, for Second Reading

Reflecting on Living the Gospel

As Jesus was being transfigured before the three apostles, their perspective was being transformed as well. When we have powerful experiences of God through worship or community, it can transform the way we see everything. We must find ways to bring those feelings with us as we descend from the mountaintop. The truth is that all of creation is imbued with the glory of God. When we experience moments of transfiguration, may we carry those moments in our hearts to remind us of the inherent goodness of life, of creation, and of God.

Making Connections

Like the gospel, the first reading shows a vision of God as a bright and fiery king in all his glory. It also hints at a trinitarian God; there is at least a Father (the "Ancient One") and a Son here. The second reading, too, speaks of the relationship between the Father and the Son. We see the early church working out its understanding of the three persons of God and how they relate to each other.

Psalmist Preparation

This psalm proclaims God as ruler over all the earth, but in our everyday lives it is not always evident that God is in charge. The psalm claims that "mountains melt like wax before the Lord," but to us mountains seem really rather permanent—as do tragedy and loss and suffering. God is a humble king and rather than make all well from a detached throne on high, he uses his power to accompany us, to walk amongst us in all our suffering. As you prepare this psalm, think of a part of your life where it is not evident that God is in control. Try to imagine God— the king of the universe—walking with you in your suffering.

Prayer

Most high over all the earth,
you are light in darkness, glory in gloom.
Each day we may witness your majesty,
if we choose to see with eyes of faith.
Help us change these glimpses of your reign
into real and tangible moments of grace.
We ask this through Jesus Christ, glorious and alive.
Amen.

AUGUST 13, 2023

Gospel (Matt 14:22-33; L115A)

After he had fed the people, Jesus made the disciples get into a boat and precede him to the other side, while he dismissed the crowds. After doing so, he went up on the mountain by himself to pray. When it was evening he was there alone. Meanwhile the boat, already a few miles offshore, was being tossed about by the waves, for the wind was against it. During the fourth watch of the night, he came toward them walking on the sea. When the disciples saw him walking on the sea they were terrified. "It is a ghost," they said, and they cried out in fear. At once

Jesus spoke to them, "Take courage, it is I; do not be afraid." Peter said to him in reply, "Lord, if it is you, command me to come to you on the water." He said, "Come." Peter got out of the boat and began to walk on the water toward Jesus. But when he saw how strong the wind was he became frightened; and, beginning to sink, he cried out, "Lord, save me!" Immediately Jesus stretched out his hand and caught Peter, and said to him, "O you of little faith, why did you doubt?" After they got into the boat, the wind died down. Those who were in the boat did him homage, saying, "Truly, you are the Son of God."

First Reading (1 Kgs 19:9a, 11-13a)

At the mountain of God, Horeb, Elijah came to a cave where he took shelter. Then the LORD said to him, "Go outside and stand on the mountain before the LORD; the LORD will be passing by." A strong and heavy wind was rending the mountains and crushing rocks before the LORD— but the LORD was not in the wind. After the wind there was an earthquake— but the LORD was not in the earthquake. After the earthquake there was fire— but the LORD was not in the fire. After the fire there was a tiny whispering sound. When he heard this, Elijah hid his face in his cloak and went and stood at the entrance of the cave.

Responsorial Psalm (Ps 85:9, 10, 11-12, 13-14)

R℣. (8) Lord, let us see your kindness, and grant us your salvation.

I will hear what God proclaims;
  the LORD—for he proclaims peace.
Near indeed is his salvation to those who fear him,
  glory dwelling in our land.

R℣. Lord, let us see your kindness, and grant us your salvation.

Kindness and truth shall meet;
  justice and peace shall kiss.
Truth shall spring out of the earth,
  and justice shall look down from heaven.

R℣. Lord, let us see your kindness, and grant us your salvation.

The LORD himself will give his benefits;
  our land shall yield its increase.
Justice shall walk before him,
  and prepare the way of his steps.

R℣. Lord, let us see your kindness, and grant us your salvation.

Second Reading (Rom 9:1-5)

Reflecting on Living the Gospel
It is to the church, to individuals and communities of disciples of "little faith," that the hand of Jesus is always outstretched to save. We too are "water walkers" today when, because of our confidence in the presence and power of Jesus, we tread the threatening waves or blustering winds that can sweep over us. Sunday after Sunday we come together to praise and adore God, despite—or perhaps because of—the storms of the past week. Like Peter, we struggle to keep faithful. Yet we come to worship him.

Making Connections
In both the first reading and the gospel, God's power is found in calmness and stillness. Elijah expects God's power to be made manifest in wind and earthquake and fire, but God is in fact found in the tiny whispering sound, one that could be missed if Elijah weren't paying attention. The gospel takes this one step further. Not only does Jesus bring stillness, he shows power over the forces of water and wind that so

frighten the disciples. God is all-powerful, yes, but God chooses to exercise this power in gentleness.

Psalmist Preparation

Like the other readings, the psalm proclaims God as one whose rulership is found in gentle ways. He proclaims not powerfully demonstrative revenge on enemies but a peace that transcends the need for vengeance. His presence is found in a good harvest, in the natural rhythms of the earth yielding abundance to provide for our needs. As you prepare to proclaim this psalm, think about the gentle ways God is present in your life. Strive to pay closer attention to at least one of these whispered hints of God's presence.

Prayer

God of Peace,
at times you speak to us not in violent storms
or in fractious earthquakes,
but in calm and gentle whispers.
Lord, let us see your kindness, and grant us your salvation.
When tempests rage and frighten us,
bring us peace, and help us trust in your unfailing power.
Amen.

Gospel (Luke 1:39-56; L622)

Mary set out and traveled to the hill country in haste to a town of Judah, where she
entered the house of Zechariah and
greeted Elizabeth. When Elizabeth heard
Mary's greeting, the infant leaped in her
womb, and Elizabeth, filled with the Holy
Spirit, cried out in a loud voice and said,
"Blessed are you among women, and
blessed is the fruit of your womb. And
how does this happen to me, that the
mother of my Lord should come to me?
For at the moment the sound of your
greeting reached my ears, the infant in

my womb leaped for joy. Blessed are you who believed that what was
spoken to you by the Lord would be fulfilled."

And Mary said:

"My soul proclaims the greatness of the Lord;
my spirit rejoices in God my Savior
for he has looked with favor upon his lowly servant.
From this day all generations will call me blessed:
the Almighty has done great things for me,
and holy is his Name.
He has mercy on those who fear him
in every generation.
He has shown the strength of his arm,
and has scattered the proud in their conceit.
He has cast down the mighty from their thrones,
and has lifted up the lowly.
He has filled the hungry with good things,
and the rich he has sent away empty.
He has come to the help of his servant Israel
for he has remembered his promise of mercy,
the promise he made to our fathers,
to Abraham and his children forever."

Mary remained with her about three months and then returned to her
home.

First Reading (Rev 11:19a; 12:1-6a, 10ab)

God's temple in heaven was opened, and the ark of his covenant could be seen in the temple.

A great sign appeared in the sky, a woman clothed with the sun, with the moon beneath her feet, and on her head a crown of twelve stars. She was with child and wailed aloud in pain as she labored to give birth. Then another sign appeared in the sky; it was a huge red dragon, with seven heads and ten horns, and on its heads were seven diadems. Its tail swept away a third of the stars in the sky and hurled them down to the earth. Then the dragon stood before the woman about to give birth, to devour her child when she gave birth. She gave birth to a son, a male child, destined to rule all the nations with an iron rod. Her child was caught up to God and his throne. The woman herself fled into the desert where she had a place prepared by God.

Then I heard a loud voice in heaven say:
"Now have salvation and power come,
and the Kingdom of our God
and the authority of his Anointed One."

Responsorial Psalm (Ps 45:10, 11, 12, 16)

R℣. (10bc) The queen stands at your right hand, arrayed in gold.

The queen takes her place at your right hand in gold of Ophir.

R℣. The queen stands at your right hand, arrayed in gold.

Hear, O daughter, and see; turn your ear,
forget your people and your father's house.

R℣. The queen stands at your right hand, arrayed in gold.

So shall the king desire your beauty;
for he is your lord.

R℣. The queen stands at your right hand, arrayed in gold.

They are borne in with gladness and joy;
they enter the palace of the king.

R℣. The queen stands at your right hand, arrayed in gold.

See Appendix, p. 218, for Second Reading

ASSUMPTION OF THE BLESSED VIRGIN MARY

Reflecting on Living the Gospel

Mary's response to God was an active one. In the *Magnificat*, which we hear in today's gospel, Mary passionately extols the virtues of God, lifting God up as a fount of justice and mercy. The God that Mary proclaims in these verses is swift, active, and shows preference to the oppressed and lowly. Are all of us, regardless of gender, being similarly responsive to God's requests to be welcomed lovingly into our bodies and lives?

Making Connections

Today's gospel describes Mary, traveling "in haste" to visit Elizabeth. To whom or what do we move "in haste" to spend time with? Do we move with haste to those things that draw us closer to God or those things that might distance ourselves from God?

Psalmist Preparation

This psalm, originally composed for a royal wedding, serves perfectly for this solemnity. Just as an ancient princess would have taken her place in splendor alongside her groom, Mary takes her place in heaven as its queen. But the Assumption is not just about Mary; it is about what is promised to all of us. She goes ahead, experiencing heaven fully, her body and soul not separated by death but remaining intact. This fullness of glory is what God wants for all of us. When the psalm says that "the king desire[s] your beauty," it is not just talking about Mary's unique beauty. It is talking to each of us. God sees each of us as uniquely and unrepeatably beautiful, and God deeply desires union with each of us. As you prepare to proclaim this Psalm, reflect on what it means that God sees you as beautiful.

Prayer

Loving God,
you chose Mary to bring to human time and space
your Eternal Word in the flesh.
Now, *[t]he queen stands at your right hand, arrayed in gold.*
When we ask for her intercession,
listen to her, our advocate and friend,
who always believed you would fulfill your promises.
Amen.

160

Gospel (Matt 15:21-28; L118A)

At that time, Jesus withdrew to the region of Tyre and Sidon. And behold, a Canaanite woman of that district came and called out, "Have pity on me, Lord, Son of David! My daughter is tormented by a demon." But Jesus did not say a word in answer to her. Jesus' disciples came and asked him, "Send her away, for she keeps calling out after us." He said in reply, "I was sent only to the lost sheep of the house of Israel." But the woman came and did Jesus homage, saying, "Lord, help me." He said in reply, "It is not right to take the food of the children and throw it to the dogs." She  said, "Please, Lord, for even the dogs eat the scraps that fall from the table of their masters." Then Jesus said to her in reply, "O woman, great is your faith! Let it be done for you as you wish." And the woman's daughter was healed from that hour.

First Reading (Isa 56:1, 6-7)

Thus says the LORD:

> Observe what is right, do what is just;
>> for my salvation is about to come,
>> my justice, about to be revealed.

> The foreigners who join themselves to the LORD,
>> ministering to him,
> loving the name of the LORD,
>> and becoming his servants—
> all who keep the sabbath free from profanation
>> and hold to my covenant,
> them I will bring to my holy mountain
>> and make joyful in my house of prayer;
> their burnt offerings and sacrifices
>> will be acceptable on my altar,
> for my house shall be called
>> a house of prayer for all peoples.

Responsorial Psalm (Ps 67:2-3, 5, 6, 8)

℟. (4) O God, let all the nations praise you!

May God have pity on us and bless us;
  may he let his face shine upon us.
So may your way be known upon earth;
  among all nations, your salvation.

℟. O God, let all the nations praise you!

May the nations be glad and exult
    because you rule the peoples in equity;
    the nations on the earth you guide.

℟. O God, let all the nations praise you!

May the peoples praise you, O God;
  may all the peoples praise you!
May God bless us,
  and may all the ends of the earth fear him!

℟. O God, let all the nations praise you!

Second Reading (Rom 11:13-15, 29-32)

Reflecting on Living the Gospel

As Matthew's predominantly Jewish Christian community struggled with the increasing number of Gentile Christians who were joining then, the evangelist could point to the incident in today's gospel reading and say, see how *Jesus himself* had to struggle with a Gentile—and see how he recognized her great faith. Not only Matthew's first-century community needs to look carefully. It is also our own racism, sexism, cultural superiority that we see reflected in this gospel. We are challenged to cross boundaries and offer them the crumbs of our compassion.

Making Connections

The first reading gives a foretaste of what we learn in the gospel: while Israel plays a special role in God's saving work, salvation is for all peoples, regardless of race or origin. The second reading, too, shows Paul striving to resolve the differences between Jews and Gentiles in his community. Both groups have a history of disobedience, but God's greater mercy is also for all.

Psalmist Preparation

The psalm very clearly echoes the message of the other readings: God is for all, for all nations and all peoples. The ultimate hope is for all to be united in praise of the one God; this end will fulfill the shared mission of Israel and of the church. As part of your preparation to proclaim this psalm, think of a story you've heard of someone who doesn't feel fully included in the church. If you don't know one, find one; the internet abounds with such stories. Pray for this person as you proclaim the psalm, that they may experience the radical hospitality of God by experiencing welcome in the church.

Prayer

O God,
let all the nations praise you!
You are just, you are welcome, you are love.
Let us never deny your gifts to others,
all created in your image and likeness,
seeking relationship with you and your holy people.
You are unity and healing for all nations.
Amen.

Gospel (Matt 16:13-20; L121A)

Jesus went into the region of Caesarea Philippi and he asked his disciples, "Who do people say that the Son of Man is?" They replied, "Some say John the Baptist, others Elijah, still others Jeremiah or one of the prophets." He said to them, "But who do you say that I am?" Simon Peter said in reply, "You are the Christ, the Son of the living God." Jesus said to him in reply, "Blessed are you, Simon son of Jonah. For flesh and blood has not revealed this to you, but my heavenly Father. And so I say to you, you are Peter, and upon this rock I will build my church, and the gates of the netherworld shall not prevail against it. I will give you the keys to the kingdom of heaven. Whatever you bind on earth shall be bound in heaven; and whatever you loose on earth shall be loosed in heaven." Then he strictly ordered his disciples to tell no one that he was the Christ.

First Reading (Isa 22:19-23)

Thus says the LORD to Shebna, master of the palace:
"I will thrust you from your office
and pull you down from your station.
On that day I will summon my servant
Eliakim, son of Hilkiah;
I will clothe him with your robe,
and gird him with your sash,
and give over to him your authority.
He shall be a father to the inhabitants of Jerusalem,
and to the house of Judah.
I will place the key of the House of David on Eliakim's shoulder;
when he opens, no one shall shut;
when he shuts, no one shall open.
I will fix him like a peg in a sure spot,
to be a place of honor for his family."

Responsorial Psalm (Ps 138:1-2, 2-3, 6, 8)

R̸. (8bc) Lord, your love is eternal; do not forsake the work of your hands.

I will give thanks to you, O LORD, with all my heart,
  for you have heard the words of my mouth;
in the presence of the angels I will sing your praise;
  I will worship at your holy temple.

R̸. Lord, your love is eternal; do not forsake the work of your hands.

I will give thanks to your name,
  because of your kindness and your truth:
when I called, you answered me;
  you built up strength within me.

R̸. Lord, your love is eternal; do not forsake the work of your hands.

The LORD is exalted, yet the lowly he sees,
  and the proud he knows from afar.
Your kindness, O LORD, endures forever;
  forsake not the work of your hands.

R̸. Lord, your love is eternal; do not forsake the work of your hands.

Second Reading (Rom 11:33-36)

Reflecting on Living the Gospel
In response to Peter's remarkable answer to Jesus's question about his identity, Jesus gives him a new name and a new mission. This "rock" became both the foundation stone of Jesus's community of disciples and ironically, later, the unstable one who, on the night of Jesus's passion, crumbled into shifting sand.

We can identify with Peter in our own weaknesses. But it will be his privilege, and the privilege of his successors in the Petrine ministry, to unlock the riches of the revelation of Jesus Christ entrusted to the church.

Making Connections
The first reading shows another instance of God delegating power to a human. It is not earned or deserved, but because God gives it, it is real. The key imagery is consistent between these readings, too; key holders have power because they are able to open and shut doors that others cannot. We don't always get to know why certain people have more power than others, and when it comes to church leadership, we are asked to trust that God holds the ultimate power and is really in control.

Psalmist Preparation

The refrain of this psalm both affirms God's eternal love and then asks God not to forsake us; it operates as if God needs from us a reminder of God's own characteristics. Of course, God does not really need this reminder, but this is a common formula for prayer. We praise something about God, then we make a request that that good thing could bring about. God is generous, so we ask for God's generosity; God is powerful, so we ask that God will exert that power on our behalf. As you prepare this psalm, think about what else you regularly find yourself asking God for. Practice prefacing your requests in prayer with a word of praise or gratitude.

Prayer

Alpha and Omega,
your love is eternal, without beginning nor end.
We are fearfully, wonderfully made in your image:
do not forsake the work of your hands.
We know not your mind and your ways;
help us always strive for greater holiness
and a stronger bond with your divine compassion.
Amen.

SEPTEMBER 3, 2023

Gospel (Matt 16:21-27; L124A)

Jesus began to show his disciples that he must go to Jerusalem and suffer greatly from the elders, the chief priests, and the scribes, and be killed and on the third day be raised. Then Peter took Jesus aside and began to rebuke him, "God forbid, Lord! No such thing shall ever happen to you." He turned and said to Peter, "Get behind me, Satan! You are an obstacle to me. You are thinking not as God does, but as human beings do."

Then Jesus said to his disciples, "Whoever wishes to come after me must deny himself, take up his cross, and follow me. For whoever wishes to save his life will lose it, but whoever loses his life for my sake will find it. What profit would there be for one to gain the whole world and forfeit his life? Or what can one give in exchange for his life? For the Son of Man will come with his angels in his Father's glory, and then he will repay all according to his conduct."

First Reading (Jer 20:7-9)

You duped me, O LORD, and I let myself be duped;
    you were too strong for me, and you triumphed.
All the day I am an object of laughter;
    everyone mocks me.

Whenever I speak, I must cry out,
    violence and outrage is my message;
the word of the LORD has brought me
    derision and reproach all the day.

I say to myself, I will not mention him,
    I will speak in his name no more.
But then it becomes like fire burning in my heart,
    imprisoned in my bones;
I grow weary holding it in, I cannot endure it.

Responsorial Psalm (Ps 63:2, 3-4, 5-6, 8-9)

℟. (2b) My soul is thirsting for you, O Lord my God.

O God, you are my God whom I seek;
    for you my flesh pines and my soul thirsts
    like the earth, parched, lifeless and without water.

℟. My soul is thirsting for you, O Lord my God.

Thus have I gazed toward you in the sanctuary
    to see your power and your glory,
for your kindness is a greater good than life;
    my lips shall glorify you.

℟. My soul is thirsting for you, O Lord my God.

Thus will I bless you while I live;
    lifting up my hands, I will call upon your name.
As with the riches of a banquet shall my soul be satisfied,
    and with exultant lips my mouth shall praise you.

℟. My soul is thirsting for you, O Lord my God.

You are my help,
    and in the shadow of your wings I shout for joy.
My soul clings fast to you;
    your right hand upholds me.

℟. My soul is thirsting for you, O Lord my God.

Second Reading (Rom 12:1-2)

Reflecting on Living the Gospel

Peter's good-hearted but false interpretation of Jesus's mission is a temptation for Jesus to follow an easier path. Peter has a long journey to make, with much blundering along the way, before he realizes the cost of following a crucified and risen Messiah. So Jesus explains not only to Peter, but to all disciples, that those who follow him will have to share his cross. This is not a call to self-destruction, but a challenge to find life by living for God and others rather than for ourselves.

Making Connections

The first reading echoes the idea that human logic is not the same as divine logic; we can feel "duped" by God when our faith brings us humiliation in the eyes of the world. But as Jeremiah finds, God has a way of drawing us back. As St. Augustine famously wrote, our hearts remain restless until they rest in God. The second reading also affirms that the life of faith involves sacrifice. We are not to conform to this world, which means it will often not feel much like home.

Psalmist Preparation

This psalm speaks of the sort of ardent desire for God that can aid us in following the gospel's call to deny ourselves and follow Christ. This intensity, though, is not always a predictable part of being a person of faith. Emotionally charged experiences are a gift, but emotions are a very fickle thing. A life of faith is rather built on disciplines, on sustainable practices that maintain our commitment even when the emotional payoff is low. As you prepare this psalm, think about times when you have shared the psalmist's passionate love for God. Think about how you live out that love when you do not feel it emotionally. Renew your commitment to some part of your practice of the faith, and know that doing so is an act of great love.

Prayer

God of the Cross,
you created each soul to yearn and pine for you,
even when that road leads to suffering and death.
To you we cry: *My soul is thirsting for you, O Lord my God.*
We thirst to love like you, serve like you;
help us to empty ourselves in service to your name.
Amen.

Gospel (Matt 18:15-20; L127A)

Jesus said to his disciples: "If your brother sins against you, go and tell him his fault between you and him alone. If he listens to you, you have won over your brother. If he does not listen, take one or two others along with you, so that 'every fact may be established on the testimony of two or three witnesses.' If he refuses to listen to them, tell the church. If he refuses to listen even to the church, then treat him as you would a Gentile or a tax collector. Amen, I say to you, whatever you bind on earth shall be bound in heaven, and whatever you loose on earth shall be loosed in heaven. Again, amen, I say to you, if two of you agree on earth about anything for which they are to pray, it shall be granted to them by my heavenly Father. For where two or three are gathered together in my name, there am I in the midst of them."

First Reading (Ezek 33:7-9)

Thus says the LORD:

> You, son of man, I have appointed watchman for the house of Israel;
> when you hear me say anything, you shall warn them for me.

If I tell the wicked, "O wicked one, you shall surely die,"

> and you do not speak out to dissuade the wicked from his way,
> the wicked shall die for his guilt,
> but I will hold you responsible for his death.

But if you warn the wicked,

> trying to turn him from his way,
> and he refuses to turn from his way,
> he shall die for his guilt,
> but you shall save yourself.

Responsorial Psalm (Ps 95:1-2, 6-7, 8-9)

℟. (8) If today you hear his voice, harden not your hearts.

Come, let us sing joyfully to the LORD;
    let us acclaim the rock of our salvation.
Let us come into his presence with thanksgiving;
    let us joyfully sing psalms to him.

℟. If today you hear his voice, harden not your hearts.

Come, let us bow down in worship;
    let us kneel before the LORD who made us.
For he is our God,
    and we are the people he shepherds, the flock he guides.

℟. If today you hear his voice, harden not your hearts.

Oh, that today you would hear his voice:
    "Harden not your hearts as at Meribah,
    as in the day of Massah in the desert,
where your fathers tempted me;
    they tested me though they had seen my works."

℟. If today you hear his voice, harden not your hearts.

Second Reading (Rom 13:8-10)

Reflecting on Living the Gospel

Forgiveness and reconciliation are one of the painful ways that we take up our cross and follow Jesus, whether in Matthew's first-century community or in today's church.

In today's gospel reading, Jesus tells his disciples how to conduct this process. The authority of "binding and loosing" that two weeks ago we heard was given to Peter to exercise in a particular way is here extended to the whole church, because it is not only the leaders who must accept responsibility for reconciliation within the community.

Making Connections

The first reading amplifies the gospel's sense of shared responsibility for sins within the community; we owe it to each other to call each other back to the Christian life. But again, our responsibility for others is limited; if they choose not to hear us, we are not called to continuously harp on what we see as their failings. And the second reading rounds out these commands; love is the context for all of this and our ultimate responsibility to each other.

Psalmist Preparation

The gospel addresses its instructions to those who need to correct another, but the psalm reminds us that we might also find ourselves on the other side of that exchange. All of us are sometimes the ones who need correction and forgiveness, and the psalm tells us to receive such correction with an open heart rather than defensiveness. As you prepare to proclaim this psalm, think of a time your behavior has been corrected, whether or not the correction was graciously delivered and whether or not you feel you deserved it. Strive to let go of any embarrassment or defensiveness surrounding this memory, and open your heart to the love that was hopefully behind it.

Prayer

God,
you sent us your Eternal Word
to show us the way to you.
You bid us: *If today you hear his voice, harden not your hearts.*
Keep our ears open and our hearts attentive,
and help us to know of your presence in our holy community.
Amen.

Gospel (Matt 18:21-35; L130A)

Peter approached Jesus and asked him, "Lord, if my brother sins against me, how often must I forgive? As many as seven times?" Jesus answered, "I say to you, not seven times but seventy-seven times. That is why the kingdom of heaven may be likened to a king who decided to settle accounts with his servants. When he began the accounting, a debtor was brought before him who owed him a huge amount. Since he had no way of paying it back, his master ordered him to be sold, along with his wife, his children, and all his property, in payment of the debt. At  that, the servant fell down, did him homage, and said, 'Be patient with me, and I will pay you back in full.' Moved with compassion the master of that servant let him go and forgave him the loan. When that servant had left, he found one of his fellow servants who owed him a much smaller amount. He seized him and started to choke him, demanding, 'Pay back what you owe.' Falling to his knees, his fellow servant begged him, 'Be patient with me, and I will pay you back.' But he refused. Instead, he had the fellow servant put in prison until he paid back the debt. Now when his fellow servants saw what had happened, they were deeply disturbed, and went to their master and reported the whole affair. His master summoned him and said to him, 'You wicked servant! I forgave you your entire debt because you begged me to. Should you not have had pity on your fellow servant, as I had pity on you?' Then in anger his master handed him over to the torturers until he should pay back the whole debt. So will my heavenly Father do to you, unless each of you forgives your brother from your heart."

First Reading (Sir 27:30–28:7)

Wrath and anger are hateful things,
    yet the sinner hugs them tight.
The vengeful will suffer the LORD's vengeance,
    for he remembers their sins in detail.

Forgive your neighbor's injustice;
>   then when you pray, your own sins will be forgiven.
Could anyone nourish anger against another
>   and expect healing from the Lord?
Could anyone refuse mercy to another like himself,
>   can he seek pardon for his own sins?
If one who is but flesh cherishes wrath,
>   who will forgive his sins?
Remember your last days, set enmity aside;
>   remember death and decay, and cease from sin!
Think of the commandments, hate not your neighbor;
>   remember the Most High's covenant, and overlook faults.

Responsorial Psalm (Ps 103:1-2, 3-4, 9-10, 11-12)

R̸. (8) The Lord is kind and merciful, slow to anger, and rich in compassion.

Bless the Lord, O my soul;
>   and all my being, bless his holy name.
Bless the Lord, O my soul,
>   and forget not all his benefits.

R̸. The Lord is kind and merciful, slow to anger, and rich in compassion.

He pardons all your iniquities,
>   heals all your ills,
redeems your life from destruction,
>   he crowns you with kindness and compassion.

R̸. The Lord is kind and merciful, slow to anger, and rich in compassion.

He will not always chide,
>   nor does he keep his wrath forever.
Not according to our sins does he deal with us,
>   nor does he requite us according to our crimes.

R̸. The Lord is kind and merciful, slow to anger, and rich in compassion.

For as the heavens are high above the earth,
>   so surpassing is his kindness toward those who fear him.
As far as the east is from the west,
>   so far has he put our transgressions from us.

R̸. The Lord is kind and merciful, slow to anger, and rich in compassion.

Second Reading (Rom 14:7-9)

Reflecting on Living the Gospel

Jesus likens membership in the kingdom of heaven to the expectation that forgiveness received from a loving and compassionate God is the basis for forgiveness offered in return to others.

To "forgive and forget" is usually a psychological contortion that is not humanly possible. The real challenge is to remember and forgive. Forgiveness is a personal demand of discipleship of Jesus, but in a world where we have experienced so much destructive bitterness between peoples, often bred from generation to generation, there is also a need for forgiveness among nations.

Making Connections

The first reading makes clear what the gospel hints at: forgiveness is a gift to the one forgiven, but it has an even more powerful impact on the one who forgives. When we refuse to forgive, it is our own hearts that become dry and hardened. Granting others the grace of forgiveness expands our own capacity to live out God's love and thus to become more truly ourselves.

Psalmist Preparation

This psalm describes the bountiful mercy of God that the gospel calls us to emulate. God always gives us more than we deserve or earn, and we are called to treat others with that same generosity. Note too that God is "slow to anger" in the first place; when we do wrong, God is not moved or changed but simply keeps responding to us in love. As you prepare the psalm this week, think of a relationship in your life that could use fuller forgiveness. Ask God for strength in moving toward deeper healing and reconciliation. Know that God promises the same for you.

Prayer

Caring Savior,
when we are angry, full of wrath and hatred,
remind us that you, holy one, are
kind and merciful, slow to anger, and rich in compassion.
Help us to forgive one another,
and enable each soul to build your reign
of justice, truth, and love.
Amen.

Gospel (Matt 20:1-16a; L133A)

Jesus told his disciples this parable: "The kingdom of heaven is like a landowner who went out at dawn to hire laborers for his vineyard. After agreeing with them for the usual daily wage, he sent them into his vineyard. Going out about nine o'clock, the landowner saw others standing idle in the marketplace, and he said to them, 'You too go into my vineyard, and I will give you what is just.' So they went off. And he went out again around noon, and around three o'clock, and did likewise. Going out about five o'clock, the landowner found others standing around, and said to them, 'Why do you stand here idle all day?' They answered, 'Because no one has hired us.' He said to them, 'You too go into my vineyard.' When it was evening the owner of the vineyard said to his foreman, 'Summon the laborers and give them their pay, beginning with the last and ending with the first.' When those who had started about five o'clock came, each received the usual daily wage. So when the first came, they thought that they would receive more, but each of them also got the usual wage. And on receiving it they grumbled against the landowner, saying, 'These last ones worked only one hour, and you have made them equal to us, who bore the day's burden and the heat.' He said to one of them in reply, 'My friend, I am not cheating you. Did you not agree with me for the usual daily wage? Take what is yours and go. What if I wish to give this last one the same as you? Or am I not free to do as I wish with my own money? Are you envious because I am generous?' Thus, the last will be first, and the first will be last."

First Reading (Isa 55:6-9)

Seek the Lord while he may be found,
    call him while he is near.
Let the scoundrel forsake his way,
    and the wicked his thoughts;
let him turn to the Lord for mercy;
    to our God, who is generous in forgiving.
For my thoughts are not your thoughts,
    nor are your ways my ways, says the Lord.

As high as the heavens are above the earth,
so high are my ways above your ways
and my thoughts above your thoughts.

Responsorial Psalm (Ps 145:2-3, 8-9, 17-18)

℟. (18a) The Lord is near to all who call upon him.

Every day will I bless you,
and I will praise your name forever and ever.
Great is the LORD and highly to be praised;
his greatness is unsearchable.

℟. The Lord is near to all who call upon him.

The LORD is gracious and merciful,
slow to anger and of great kindness.
The LORD is good to all
and compassionate toward all his works.

℟. The Lord is near to all who call upon him.

The LORD is just in all his ways
and holy in all his works.
The LORD is near to all who call upon him,
to all who call upon him in truth.

℟. The Lord is near to all who call upon him.

Second Reading (Phil 1:20c-24, 27a)

Reflecting on Living the Gospel

As we listen to this parable as a eucharistic community, we are powerfully reminded of the equality and solidarity of all God's laboring disciples who receive the same food at the same table. Yet are there people about whose presence we are judgmental? And outside of Mass, is our vision of our brothers and sisters darkened by envy, and even by an unexpressed suspicion of or open grumbling about God who seems to be unfair with his generosity—especially to me? Does making comparisons override being in communion?

Making Connections

The first reading reminds us in no uncertain terms that God's ways are not our ways. God operates on a different kind of logic, one which surpasses everything we would call logical but rather operates out of a love that overflows with life-giving power. As St. Paul voices in the second reading, we are called to imitate God's ongoing self-gift. We can be united to Christ in both life and death when we strive to follow his example.

Psalmist Preparation

This psalm refrain shows the stunning generosity of God; to be near to God, all we need to do is call. God is already there awaiting our appeal. It's not as mind-bending an image as the gospel, but it's the same breath-taking truth: God's generosity far exceeds anything we could expect or imagine. As you prepare this psalm, reflect on what it means to you for God to be near. How do you know God's closeness? Are there times it is it hard to perceive? Try to find a moment or two this week that can serve as evidence of God's personal love for you, and proclaim this psalm as a prayer of thanksgiving for those moments.

Prayer

Omnipotent God, Immanent God,
you are *near to all who call upon* you,
grace and mercy to each heart in need.
Keep us humble, trusting in the mystery that is you;
help us live the paradox that power is service,
being first is being last, and that in death is new life.
Amen.

OCTOBER 1, 2023

Gospel (Matt 21:28-32; L136A)

Jesus said to the chief priests and elders of the people: "What is your opinion? A man had two sons. He came to the first and said, 'Son, go out and work in the vineyard today.' He said in reply, 'I will not,' but afterwards changed his mind and went. The man came to the other son and gave the same order. He said in reply, 'Yes, sir,' but did not go. Which of the two did his father's will?" They answered, "The first." Jesus said to them, "Amen, I say to you, tax collectors and prostitutes are entering the kingdom of God before you. When John came to you in the way of righteousness,  you did not believe him; but tax collectors and prostitutes did. Yet even when you saw that, you did not later change your minds and believe him."

First Reading (Ezek 18:25-28)

Thus says the LORD:
You say, "The LORD's way is not fair!"
Hear now, house of Israel:
   Is it my way that is unfair, or rather, are not your ways unfair?
When someone virtuous turns away from virtue to commit iniquity,
      and dies,
   it is because of the iniquity he committed that he must die.
But if he turns from the wickedness he has committed,
      and does what is right and just,
   he shall preserve his life;
      since he has turned away from all the sins that he has committed,
      he shall surely live, he shall not die.

Responsorial Psalm (Ps 25:4-5, 6-7, 8-9)

R̿. (6a) Remember your mercies, O Lord.

Your ways, O LORD, make known to me;
    teach me your paths,
guide me in your truth and teach me,
    for you are God my savior.

R̿. Remember your mercies, O Lord.

Remember that your compassion, O LORD,
    and your love are from of old.
The sins of my youth and my frailties remember not;
    in your kindness remember me,
    because of your goodness, O LORD.

R̿. Remember your mercies, O Lord.

Good and upright is the LORD;
    thus he shows sinners the way.
He guides the humble to justice,
    and teaches the humble his way.

R̿. Remember your mercies, O Lord.

Second Reading (Phil 2:1-11 [or Phil 2:1-5])

Reflecting on Living the Gospel

Jesus's parable today reminds us of how easy it is to say an initial "yes" when fervor is high, failure seems impossible, and the future looks golden. But time passes, the enthusiasms cool, the relationships that have to endure through the long haul of married love, the promises of friendship or vocation, have to be truthfully discerned and embraced every day, and the original "yes" is repeated—not with an initial blaze but with the burning embers that are daily fanned by our fidelity, in good times and bad.

Making Connections

The first reading stresses again that God does not think like us; divine logic is based on love. Our human notions of "fairness" are only marginally related to the true justice that God is bringing about. The second reading takes up a similar theme; we are not only to love others as ourselves but to see them as *more* important than we are. This is illogical and does not fit into the human way of being in the world, but it imitates the lavish love that God offers to all of us.

Psalmist Preparation

Note who God teaches in the last verse of this psalm: it is the humble who God guides to justice and to whom God teaches his way. Those who are proud are not able to receive guidance, for they believe they know what they need to know and so their hearts are hardened to learning more. Those who are humble are able to receive God's guidance and teaching; their hearts are oriented to learn. As you prepare this psalm, reflect on what humility means to you. How can you cultivate this virtue so that you might be more receptive to what God wants to teach you?

Prayer

God of life,
you teach us to empty ourselves,
and not cling to power or influence.
You reach out to sinners,
asking them to transform their hearts,
and return to you.
Remember your mercies, O Lord.
Give us strength to turn away from sin
and to be faithful to your good news.
Amen.

Gospel (Matt 21:33-43; L139A)

Jesus said to the chief priests and the elders of the people: "Hear another parable. There was a landowner who planted a vineyard, put a hedge around it, dug a wine press in it, and built a tower. Then he leased it to tenants and went on a journey. When vintage time drew near, he sent his servants to the tenants to obtain his produce. But the tenants seized the servants and one they beat, another they killed, and a third they stoned. Again he sent other servants, more numerous than the first ones, but they treated them in the same way. Finally, he

sent his son to them, thinking, 'They will respect my son.' But when the tenants saw the son, they said to one another, 'This is the heir. Come, let us kill him and acquire his inheritance.' They seized him, threw him out of the vineyard, and killed him. What will the owner of the vineyard do to those tenants when he comes?" They answered him, "He will put those wretched men to a wretched death and lease his vineyard to other tenants who will give him the produce at the proper times." Jesus said to them, "Did you never read in the Scriptures:

The stone that the builders rejected
has become the cornerstone;
by the Lord has this been done,
and it is wonderful in our eyes?

Therefore, I say to you, the kingdom of God will be taken away from you and given to a people that will produce its fruit."

First Reading (Isa 5:1-7)

Let me now sing of my friend,
 my friend's song concerning his vineyard.
My friend had a vineyard
 on a fertile hillside;
he spaded it, cleared it of stones,
 and planted the choicest vines;
within it he built a watchtower,
 and hewed out a wine press.

Then he looked for the crop of grapes,
   but what it yielded was wild grapes.

Now, inhabitants of Jerusalem and people of Judah,
   judge between me and my vineyard:
What more was there to do for my vineyard
   that I had not done?
Why, when I looked for the crop of grapes,
   did it bring forth wild grapes?
Now, I will let you know
   what I mean to do with my vineyard:
take away its hedge, give it to grazing,
   break through its wall, let it be trampled!
Yes, I will make it a ruin:
   it shall not be pruned or hoed,
   but overgrown with thorns and briers;
I will command the clouds
   not to send rain upon it.
The vineyard of the Lord of hosts is the house of Israel,
   and the people of Judah are his cherished plant;
he looked for judgment, but see, bloodshed!
   for justice, but hark, the outcry!

Responsorial Psalm (Ps 80:9, 12, 13-14, 15-16, 19-20)

℟. (Isaiah 5:7a) The vineyard of the Lord is the house of Israel.

A vine from Egypt you transplanted;
   you drove away the nations and planted it.
It put forth its foliage to the Sea,
   its shoots as far as the River.

℟. The vineyard of the Lord is the house of Israel.

Why have you broken down its walls,
   so that every passer-by plucks its fruit,
the boar from the forest lays it waste,
   and the beasts of the field feed upon it?

℟. The vineyard of the Lord is the house of Israel.

Once again, O Lord of hosts,
　　look down from heaven, and see;
take care of this vine,
　　and protect what your right hand has planted,
　　the son of man whom you yourself made strong.

R̸. The vineyard of the Lord is the house of Israel.

Then we will no more withdraw from you;
　　give us new life, and we will call upon your name.
O Lord, God of hosts, restore us;
　　if your face shine upon us, then we shall be saved.

R̸. The vineyard of the Lord is the house of Israel.

Second Reading (Phil 4:6-9)

Reflecting on Living the Gospel

Today's parable stresses the need to bear fruit. It offers a warning to those who are unproductive and bear no fruit, especially at vintage time when the Son of Man will come to claim the harvest of our lives. Are we possessive rebels who want people and possessions to serve our own ambitions, with no thought of serving others? Can we honestly recognize that by our hypocrisy or integrity, our deafness to the prophets in our own times, we run the risk of becoming self-condemned tenants of God's vineyard?

Making Connections

The first reading echoes the vineyard imagery that has been so strong in the gospels of the past several weeks. Israel is the vineyard that God refuses to give up on; life and love will win out over human failure to participate in them. The second reading balances the anxiety that might be produced by the harsh judgments of the other readings. Paul reassures us that God is a God of peace, who remains with us whenever we choose what is true and good and beautiful.

Psalmist Preparation

This psalm reminds us of the ever-enduring faithfulness of God. Composed during a time of exile, this psalm expresses confidence in God's desire to love us and make us fruitful, even when we have failed to do so in the past. Even when all seems lost, God is on our side, never willing to fully abandon those he created out of love. This psalm calls on God to offer another chance, to enact the abundant generosity we have seen in so many of the readings of these last weeks. As you prepare this psalm, think about where you need God's generosity to become more apparent in your life. Bring your needs and desires fully before God in prayer; God can handle even the pain with which you might bring them. Sing these verses with the yearning of Israel far from home, longing to be reunited with God's special presence in the temple.

Prayer

God of the Harvest,
you call us to tend what you have planted,
reminding us that *[t]he vineyard of the Lord is the house of Israel.*
May our labors bring your Church to flourish and prosper,
and yield much fruit for the building of your reign
and the glory of your name.
Amen.

Gospel (Matt 22:1-14
[or Matt 22:1-10]; L142A)

Jesus again in reply spoke to the chief priests and elders of the people in parables, saying, "The kingdom of heaven may be likened to a king who gave a wedding feast for his son. He dispatched his servants to summon the invited guests to the feast, but they refused to come. A second time he sent other servants, saying, 'Tell those invited: "Behold, I have prepared my banquet, my calves and fattened cattle are killed, and everything is ready; come to the feast."' Some ignored the invitation and went away, one to his farm, another to his business. The rest laid hold of his servants, mistreated them, and killed them. The king was enraged and sent his troops, destroyed those murderers, and burned their city. Then he said to his servants, 'The feast is ready, but those who were invited were not worthy to come. Go out, therefore, into the main roads and invite to the feast whomever you find.' The servants went out into the streets and gathered all they found, bad and good alike, and the hall was filled with guests. But when the king came in to meet the guests, he saw a man there not dressed in a wedding garment. The king said to him, 'My friend, how is it that you came in here without a wedding garment?' But he was reduced to silence. Then the king said to his attendants, 'Bind his hands and feet, and cast him into the darkness outside, where there will be wailing and grinding of teeth.' Many are invited, but few are chosen."

First Reading (Isa 25:6-10a)

On this mountain the LORD of hosts
    will provide for all peoples
a feast of rich food and choice wines,
    juicy, rich food and pure, choice wines.
On this mountain he will destroy
    the veil that veils all peoples,
the web that is woven over all nations;
    he will destroy death forever.

The Lord GOD will wipe away
  the tears from every face;
the reproach of his people he will remove
  from the whole earth; for the LORD has spoken.
  On that day it will be said:
"Behold our God, to whom we looked to save us!
  This is the LORD for whom we looked;
  let us rejoice and be glad that he has saved us!"
For the hand of the LORD will rest on this mountain.

Responsorial Psalm (Ps 23:1-3a, 3b-4, 5, 6)

R̸. (6cd) I shall live in the house of the Lord all the days of my life.

The LORD is my shepherd; I shall not want.
  In verdant pastures he gives me repose;
beside restful waters he leads me;
  he refreshes my soul.

R̸. I shall live in the house of the Lord all the days of my life.

He guides me in right paths
  for his name's sake.
Even though I walk in the dark valley
  I fear no evil; for you are at my side
with your rod and your staff
  that give me courage.

R̸. I shall live in the house of the Lord all the days of my life.

You spread the table before me
  in the sight of my foes;
you anoint my head with oil;
  my cup overflows.

R̸. I shall live in the house of the Lord all the days of my life.

Only goodness and kindness follow me
  all the days of my life;
and I shall dwell in the house of the LORD
  for years to come.

R̸. I shall live in the house of the Lord all the days of my life.

Second Reading (Phil 4:12-14, 19-20)

Reflecting on Living the Gospel

As a church, we too are servants sent out to invite others, and we'll receive some indifference and sometimes even persecution in return. But we are also the invited guests. Do we reject the invitation because of other priorities: personal success, selfishness, materialism, fear of judgment of others? At the feast of the Eucharist, do we just show up, ignoring the other guests, not caring if we are clothed in love? And does all this make our baptismal clothing tattered and grubby, unfit for a holy feast?

Making Connections

The first reading gives us a foretaste of the gospel's feast: God provides and God provides abundantly. We are not provided just the bread and water we need to live; this is a tasty, lavish feast. It tends to not just our bare physical needs but to our emotional ones, too: God removes our guilt and wipes away our tears. The second reading also assures us of, God's providence; God has all we need (and all we could ever want) and God's "glorious riches" are there to provide for our needs.

Psalmist Preparation

We've heard this psalm several times throughout the liturgical year; it echoes this week's other readings as another beautiful image of the abundant care God has for us. God promises us fullness and rest and vibrant, plentiful life. Our final goal is life with God, a life in which all our needs will be cared for and tended to. As part of your preparation to proclaim this psalm, be sure to spend some time with the other readings for the week to round out your image of the abundant feast that God prepares and wills for all of us. Spend some prayer time envisioning yourself in these scenes.

Prayer

Good Shepherd,
you provide all that we need,
and sustain us through hunger, sadness,
and our need for redemption.
Seeing you one day face-to-face, move us to exclaim:
I shall live in the house of the Lord all the days of my life.
The fullness of joys, in your presence, are wonderful indeed.
Amen.

OCTOBER 22, 2023

Gospel **(Matt 22:15-21; L145A)**

The Pharisees went off and plotted how they might entrap Jesus in speech. They sent their disciples to him, with the Herodians, saying, "Teacher, we know that you are a truthful man and that you teach the way of God in accordance with the truth. And you are not concerned with anyone's opinion, for you do not regard a person's status. Tell us, then, what is your opinion: Is it lawful to pay the census tax to Caesar or not?" Knowing their malice, Jesus said, "Why are you testing me, you hypocrites? Show me the coin that pays the census tax." Then they handed him the Roman coin. He said to them, "Whose image is this and whose inscription?" They replied, "Caesar's." At that he said to them, "Then repay to Caesar what belongs to Caesar and to God what belongs to God."

First Reading **(Isa 45:1, 4-6)**

Thus says the LORD to his anointed, Cyrus,
    whose right hand I grasp,
subduing nations before him,
    and making kings run in his service,
opening doors before him
    and leaving the gates unbarred:
For the sake of Jacob, my servant,
    of Israel, my chosen one,
I have called you by your name,
    giving you a title, though you knew me not.
I am the LORD and there is no other,
    there is no God besides me.
It is I who arm you, though you know me not,
    so that toward the rising and the setting of the sun
    people may know that there is none besides me.
I am the LORD, there is no other.

Responsorial Psalm (Ps 96:1, 3, 4-5, 7-8, 9-10)

R̂. (7b) Give the Lord glory and honor.

Sing to the LORD a new song;
    sing to the LORD, all you lands.
Tell his glory among the nations;
    among all peoples, his wondrous deeds.

R̂. Give the Lord glory and honor.

For great is the LORD and highly to be praised;
    awesome is he, beyond all gods.
For all the gods of the nations are things of nought,
    but the LORD made the heavens.

R̂. Give the Lord glory and honor.

Give to the LORD, you families of nations,
    give to the LORD glory and praise;
    give to the LORD the glory due his name!
Bring gifts, and enter his courts.

R̂. Give the Lord glory and honor.

Worship the LORD, in holy attire;
    tremble before him, all the earth;
say among the nations: The LORD is king,
    he governs the peoples with equity.

R̂. Give the Lord glory and honor.

Second Reading (1 Thess 1:1-5b)

Reflecting on Living the Gospel

Jesus's "Repay to Caesar what belongs to Caesar and to God what belongs to God" reminds us that Christian disciples need to discern how to live in history and society while maintaining our commitment to the reign of God. Jesus does not elaborate on the "how" to do this. He leaves that up to people in their own distinct times and places.

Where is God's impression in the "coinage" of our daily life? The answer is: on everything that God has made, and especially on other people.

Making Connections

Like the gospel, the first reading makes an important distinction between earthly and divine power. Human leaders may do good work that is willed by God, but God affirms that "I am the Lord and there is no other, there is no God besides me." No other power, no matter how good, can fulfill what is God's to fulfill.

Psalmist Preparation

"Give the Lord glory and honor." Implied in this psalm's outpouring of praise is that it is *only* God who deserves this glory and honor. God's power is ultimate, above all others, and God deserves our whole hearts and our utmost in love and loyalty. As you prepare this psalm, reflect on those things in your life that threaten to become idols—that is, those things that run the risk of taking the place in your heart that ought to belong only to God. Make a resolution to distance yourself from one of these things in some small way this week so that there is more room in your heart to sincerely proclaim the praises of this psalm.

Prayer

God of Majesty and Might,
there is none like you, kind and understanding,
wise and forgiving.
Therefore, we *give* you *glory and honor,*
we praise your name and your mighty arm,
giving good things to the lowly,
and casting down those who cling to earthly power.
Amen.

Gospel (Matt 22:34-40; L148A)

When the Pharisees heard that Jesus had silenced the Sadducees, they gathered together, and one of them, a scholar of the law, tested him by asking, "Teacher, which commandment in the law is the greatest?" He said to him, "You shall love the Lord, your God, with all your heart, with all your soul, and with all your mind. This is the greatest and the first commandment. The second is like it: You shall love your neighbor as yourself. The whole law and the prophets depend on these two commandments."

First Reading (Exod 22:20-26)

Thus says the LORD:
"You shall not molest or oppress an alien,
  for you were once aliens yourselves in the land of Egypt.
You shall not wrong any widow or orphan.
If ever you wrong them and they cry out to me,
  I will surely hear their cry.
My wrath will flare up, and I will kill you with the sword;
  then your own wives will be widows, and your children orphans.

"If you lend money to one of your poor neighbors among my people,
  you shall not act like an extortioner toward him
  by demanding interest from him.
If you take your neighbor's cloak as a pledge,
  you shall return it to him before sunset;
  for this cloak of his is the only covering he has for his body.
What else has he to sleep in?
If he cries out to me, I will hear him; for I am compassionate."

Responsorial Psalm (Ps 18:2-3, 3-4, 47, 51)

R̞. (2) I love you, Lord, my strength.

I love you, O LORD, my strength,
  O LORD, my rock, my fortress, my deliverer.

R̞. I love you, Lord, my strength.

My God, my rock of refuge,
 my shield, the horn of my salvation, my stronghold!
Praised be the Lord, I exclaim,
 and I am safe from my enemies.

R̸. I love you, Lord, my strength.

The Lord lives and blessed be my rock!
 Extolled be God my savior.
You who gave great victories to your king
 and showed kindness to your anointed.

R̸. I love you, Lord, my strength.

Second Reading (1 Thess 1:5c-10)

Reflecting on Living the Gospel

Challenged to name the greatest commandment among the 613 precepts of the Mosaic Torah, Jesus cites two: one commanding the love of God "with all your heart, with all your soul, and with all your mind" (see Deut 6:4-9), the other commanding love of neighbor (see Lev 19:18).

Everything, Jesus says, hangs on these. A door hangs on two hinges; if one is out of alignment, it won't swing properly or open easily. If love of God and neighbor are out of balance, our lives will be badly aligned.

Making Connections

The first reading shows that the God of the Old Testament is not some being foreign from the Jesus of the New Testament. The love that Jesus preaches does not *replace* the law. There is continuity here. God's Old Testament commandments are more specific, and make punishment clearer, but they are about the very love for neighbor that Jesus has named as so important. To treat foreigners and widows and orphans with justice is to fulfill the love to which we are called.

Psalmist Preparation

In this psalm we sing of the love for God to which the gospel calls us. We also affirm that we are not called to give ourselves to God one-sidedly; we name here many of the things that God is for us. In this psalm, God is named as our "strength," "rock," "fortress," "deliverer," "shield," "horn of . . . salvation," "stronghold"—and this is just a small selection of the names for God we find in the Bible and in the Christian tradition. As you prepare this psalm, choose one of these titles to sit with. How does it resonate with your image of God? How does it challenge it or help it to expand?

Prayer

God of Wayfarers,
you are welcome to the stranger,
and wonderful bounty to those in need.
May those we meet who need our help
know you through our acts of loving service,
and be compelled, in joy and gratitude,
to praise your name: *I love you, Lord, my strength.*
Amen.

Gospel (Matt 5:1-12a; L667)

When Jesus saw the crowds, he went up the mountain, and after he had sat down, his disciples came to him. He began to teach them, saying:

"Blessed are the poor in spirit,
for theirs is the Kingdom of heaven.
Blessed are they who mourn,
for they will be comforted.
Blessed are the meek,
for they will inherit the land.
Blessed are they who hunger and thirst
for righteousness,
for they will be satisfied.
Blessed are the merciful,
for they will be shown mercy.
Blessed are the clean of heart,
for they will see God.
Blessed are the peacemakers,
for they will be called children of God.
Blessed are they who are persecuted for the sake of righteousness,
for theirs is the Kingdom of heaven.

Blessed are you when they insult you and persecute you and utter every kind of evil against you falsely because of me. Rejoice and be glad, for your reward will be great in heaven."

First Reading (Rev 7:2-4, 9-14)

I, John, saw another angel come up from the East, holding the seal of the living God. He cried out in a loud voice to the four angels who were given power to damage the land and the sea, "Do not damage the land or the sea or the trees until we put the seal on the foreheads of the servants of our God." I heard the number of those who had been marked with the seal, one hundred and forty-four thousand marked from every tribe of the children of Israel.

After this I had a vision of a great multitude, which no one could count, from every nation, race, people, and tongue. They stood before the throne and before the Lamb, wearing white robes and holding palm branches in their hands. They cried out in a loud voice:

"Salvation comes from our God,
    who is seated on the throne,
and from the Lamb."

All the angels stood around the throne and around the elders and the
four living creatures. They prostrated themselves before the throne,
worshiped God, and exclaimed:

"Amen. Blessing and glory, wisdom and thanksgiving,
    honor, power, and might
    be to our God forever and ever. Amen."

Then one of the elders spoke up and said to me, "Who are these wearing
white robes, and where did they come from?" I said to him, "My lord, you
are the one who knows." He said to me, "These are the ones who have
survived the time of great distress; they have washed their robes and
made them white in the Blood of the Lamb."

Responsorial Psalm (Ps 24:1-2, 3–4ab, 5-6)

R̶. (cf. 6) Lord, this is the people that longs to see your face.

The LORD's are the earth and its fullness;
    the world and those who dwell in it.
For he founded it upon the seas
    and established it upon the rivers.

R̶. Lord, this is the people that longs to see your face.

Who can ascend the mountain of the LORD?
    or who may stand in his holy place?
One whose hands are sinless, whose heart is clean,
    who desires not what is vain.

R̶. Lord, this is the people that longs to see your face.

He shall receive a blessing from the LORD,
    a reward from God his savior.
Such is the race that seeks for him,
    that seeks the face of the God of Jacob.

R̶. Lord, this is the people that longs to see your face.

See Appendix, p. 218, for Second Reading

Reflecting on Living the Gospel

Mastery-based learning is an educational framework in which students are expected to demonstrate deep understanding, or mastery, of a topic before moving on to the next one. Students who learn in mastery-based settings are encouraged to embrace the power of "yet," to cultivate the belief that with time, consistent practice, and constructive feedback from a trusted guide they can improve their knowledge and skills. The solemnity of All Saints is one that invites believers to assume a growth mindset, to embrace the power of "yet" with regard to our spiritual lives.

Making Connections

While the Beatitudes offer the hope and promise of God's kingdom, we also recognize that right now there are many people who are poor, people who hunger, and people who mourn. These are not easy realities. If we wish to join the communion of saints, we must be willing to see the face of God in ourselves and others, turning toward the poor, hungry, hurting, and lonely in our community, rather than away from them.

Psalmist Preparation

This psalm's second verse can read like a checklist for sanctity, and an unattainable one at that. It might sound like we need to achieve "sinless hands" and a "clean heart" before we can stand with God. But the final verse reminds us that sanctity is really about seeking. It is not about accomplishments but about dedication to a journey. Saints are not those who achieve anything in particular in this life; saints are those who keep longing for and striving after God. The specifics of their journeys do not fit any checklist; they are glorious in their diversity. As you prepare this psalm, reflect on your own call to sainthood. What does holiness look like in the particulars of your unique life?

Prayer

Lord of Heaven and Earth,
hide not your presence from us:
Lord, this is the people that longs to see your face.
Bring us to be more like you,
pure and holy,
and bring us, poor in spirit,
into your reign of peace, mercy, and righteousness.
Amen.

Gospel (Matt 23:1-12; L151A)

Jesus spoke to the crowds and to his disciples, saying, "The scribes and the Pharisees have taken their seat on the chair of Moses. Therefore, do and observe all things whatsoever they tell you, but do not follow their example. For they preach but they do not practice. They tie up heavy burdens hard to carry and lay them on people's shoulders, but they will not lift a finger to move them. All their works are performed to be seen. They widen their phylacteries and lengthen their tassels. They love places of honor at  banquets, seats of honor in synagogues, greetings in marketplaces, and the salutation 'Rabbi.' As for you, do not be called 'Rabbi.' You have but one teacher, and you are all brothers. Call no one on earth your father; you have but one Father in heaven. Do not be called 'Master'; you have but one master, the Christ. The greatest among you must be your servant. Whoever exalts himself will be humbled; but whoever humbles himself will be exalted."

First Reading (Mal 1:14b–2:2b, 8-10)

A great King am I, says the LORD of hosts,
> and my name will be feared among the nations.
And now, O priests, this commandment is for you:
> If you do not listen,
if you do not lay it to heart,
> to give glory to my name, says the LORD of hosts,
I will send a curse upon you
> and of your blessing I will make a curse.
You have turned aside from the way,
> and have caused many to falter by your instruction;
you have made void the covenant of Levi,
> says the LORD of hosts.
I, therefore, have made you contemptible
> and base before all the people,
since you do not keep my ways,
> but show partiality in your decisions.

Have we not all the one father?
Has not the one God created us?
Why then do we break faith with one another,
violating the covenant of our fathers?

Responsorial Psalm (Ps 131:1, 2, 3)

℟. In you, Lord, I have found my peace.

O LORD, my heart is not proud,
nor are my eyes haughty;
I busy not myself with great things,
nor with things too sublime for me.

℟. In you, Lord, I have found my peace.

Nay rather, I have stilled and quieted
my soul like a weaned child.
Like a weaned child on its mother's lap,
so is my soul within me.

℟. In you, Lord, I have found my peace.

O Israel, hope in the LORD,
both now and forever.

℟. In you, Lord, I have found my peace.

Second Reading (1 Thess 2:7b-9, 13)

Reflecting on Living the Gospel
In today's gospel, Jesus criticizes the way many Jewish leaders of his day clung to titles of honor and power, seized the limelight, and were attached to ostentatious religious garb. If we are inclined to dismiss these criticisms as rather quaint and irrelevant, we might consider the meaning of titles like *Eminence, Excellency,* or *Monsignor* (literally, "my Lord") or expensive dwellings and insignia for some clergy—all of which are common aspects of Catholic life.

Making Connections
Both the psalm and the second reading use images of being cared for as a mother cares for her children; in the psalm it is an image for God's care for us, and in Thessalonians it is an image for how church leaders ought to care for the flock entrusted to them. This is again a reversal of our expectations: the self-giving work of mothers often goes unseen and unacknowledged, yet it is here a mark of leadership.

Psalmist Preparation

You might see some wry smiles from mothers this week when you sing about the still, quiet child on its mother's lap—if the mothers in your congregation even have a chance to hear the words you're singing! As you prepare this psalm, say a prayer for all the parents who will hear it while wrangling small children through Mass. They are icons of the humility to which the gospel calls us, and they could likely use the peace the psalmist has found. Pray, too, for their children, who may still be learning how to behave in church but who are also the face of Christ to all of us present.

Prayer

Gentle and Compassionate God,
when troubles weigh us down
and storms disturb our well-being,
put this prayer on our lips:
In you, Lord, I have found my peace.
For only you have true peace, that which the world cannot give.
Grant us humility and rest, and serene hope in your presence.
Amen.

NOVEMBER 12, 2023

Gospel (Matt 25:1-13; L154A)

Jesus told his disciples this parable: "The kingdom of heaven will be like ten virgins who took their lamps and went out to meet the bridegroom. Five of them were foolish and five were wise. The foolish ones, when taking their lamps, brought no oil with them, but the wise brought flasks of oil with their lamps. Since the bridegroom was long delayed, they all became drowsy and fell asleep. At midnight, there was a cry, 'Behold, the bridegroom! Come out to meet him!' Then all those virgins got up and trimmed their lamps. The foolish ones said to the wise, 'Give us

some of your oil, for our lamps are going out.' But the wise ones replied, 'No, for there may not be enough for us and you. Go instead to the merchants and buy some for yourselves.' While they went off to buy it, the bridegroom came and those who were ready went into the wedding feast with him. Then the door was locked. Afterwards the other virgins came and said, 'Lord, Lord, open the door for us!' But he said in reply, 'Amen, I say to you, I do not know you.' Therefore, stay awake, for you know neither the day nor the hour."

First Reading (Wis 6:12-16)

Resplendent and unfading is wisdom,
    and she is readily perceived by those who love her,
    and found by those who seek her.
She hastens to make herself known in anticipation of their desire;
    whoever watches for her at dawn shall not be disappointed,
    for he shall find her sitting by his gate.
For taking thought of wisdom is the perfection of prudence,
    and whoever for her sake keeps vigil
    shall quickly be free from care;
because she makes her own rounds, seeking those worthy of her,
    and graciously appears to them in the ways,
    and meets them with all solicitude.

Responsorial Psalm (Ps 63:2, 3-4, 5-6, 7-8)

℟. (2b) My soul is thirsting for you, O Lord my God.

O God, you are my God whom I seek;
>for you my flesh pines and my soul thirsts
>like the earth, parched, lifeless and without water.

℟. My soul is thirsting for you, O Lord my God.

Thus have I gazed toward you in the sanctuary
>to see your power and your glory,
for your kindness is a greater good than life;
>my lips shall glorify you.

℟. My soul is thirsting for you, O Lord my God.

Thus will I bless you while I live;
>lifting up my hands, I will call upon your name.
As with the riches of a banquet shall my soul be satisfied,
>and with exultant lips my mouth shall praise you.

℟. My soul is thirsting for you, O Lord my God.

I will remember you upon my couch,
>and through the night-watches I will meditate on you:
you are my help,
>and in the shadow of your wings I shout for joy.

℟. My soul is thirsting for you, O Lord my God.

Second Reading (1 Thess 4:13-18 [or 1 Thess 4:13-14])

Reflecting on Living the Gospel

Uniquely, the parable we hear today portrays discipleship in feminine imagery. Although the parable is primarily concerned with what lies behind the, as yet, closed doors of the end of cosmic history and Christ's second coming, the Bridegroom will also come to us in our own death. One Eucharist will be the last from which we take the oil from the two tables of word and sacrament that help us to keep our lamps burning and light our way to open the doors of our hearts to the Bridegroom.

Making Connections

The second reading reminds us that, even in the face of all that is dark and scary in the world, we are called to live with hope—hope granted to us through faith in the one who has conquered even death. The first reading tells us more about the wisdom attributed to half the gospel's virgins; this wisdom character is also read as an Old Testament image of Christ. Here, she is not a hardhearted host but is always waiting and preparing for those who seek her. Our love for wisdom—and for Jesus, the wisdom of God—is always met with preexisting love that seeks us first.

Psalmist Preparation

This is one of the most heart-wrenchingly passionate psalms we sing as a church. The image of the parched earth is powerful; its readiness to receive and absorb rain is the posture we are asked to possess toward Christ both at his final coming and in all his everyday comings into our hearts and lives. This psalm is especially powerful at Mass as we move toward the Liturgy of the Eucharist; our flesh pines and our soul thirsts, and God responds with giving us his flesh and his blood for drink. Try to bring this psalm into your preparation for and reception of the Eucharist this week, receiving Christ with the ardent love of which the psalmist sings here.

Prayer

Wellspring of Eternal Life,
you who are refreshment and vivification,
our souls are *thirsting for you, O Lord.*
Lead us to drink of you who satisfy all desires,
and, revived, keep us watchful and alert for your coming.
Make us ready to greet you at your coming.
Amen.

Gospel (Matt 25:14-30 [or Matt 25:14-15, 19-21]; L157A)

Jesus told his disciples this parable: "A man going on a journey called in his servants and entrusted his possessions to them. To one he gave five talents; to another, two; to a third, one— to each according to his ability. Then he went away. Immediately the one who received five talents went and traded with them, and made another five. Likewise, the one who received two made another two. But the man who received one went off and dug a hole in the ground and buried his master's money.

"After a long time the master of those servants came back and settled accounts with them. The one who had received five talents came forward bringing the additional five. He said, 'Master, you gave me five talents. See, I have made five more.' His master said to him, 'Well done, my good and faithful servant. Since you were faithful in small matters, I will give you great responsibilities. Come, share your master's joy.' Then the one who had received two talents also came forward and said, 'Master, you gave me two talents. See, I have made two more.' His master said to him, 'Well done, my good and faithful servant. Since you were faithful in small matters, I will give you great responsibilities. Come, share your master's joy.' Then the one who had received the one talent came forward and said, 'Master, I knew you were a demanding person, harvesting where you did not plant and gathering where you did not scatter; so out of fear I went off and buried your talent in the ground. Here it is back.' His master said to him in reply, 'You wicked, lazy servant! So you knew that I harvest where I did not plant and gather where I did not scatter? Should you not then have put my money in the bank so that I could have got it back with interest on my return? Now then! Take the talent from him and give it to the one with ten. For to everyone who has, more will be given and he will grow rich; but from the one who has not, even what he has will be taken away. And throw this useless servant into the darkness outside, where there will be wailing and grinding of teeth.'"

First Reading (Prov 31:10-13, 19-20, 30-31)

When one finds a worthy wife,
    her value is far beyond pearls.
Her husband, entrusting his heart to her,
    has an unfailing prize.
She brings him good, and not evil,
    all the days of her life.
She obtains wool and flax
    and works with loving hands.
She puts her hands to the distaff,
    and her fingers ply the spindle.
She reaches out her hands to the poor,
    and extends her arms to the needy.
Charm is deceptive and beauty fleeting;
    the woman who fears the Lord is to be praised.
Give her a reward for her labors,
    and let her works praise her at the city gates.

Responsorial Psalm (Ps 128:1-2, 3, 4-5)

℟. (cf. 1a) Blessed are those who fear the Lord.

Blessed are you who fear the Lord,
    who walk in his ways!
For you shall eat the fruit of your handiwork;
    blessed shall you be, and favored.

℟. Blessed are those who fear the Lord.

Your wife shall be like a fruitful vine
    in the recesses of your home;
your children like olive plants
    around your table.

℟. Blessed are those who fear the Lord.

Behold, thus is the man blessed
    who fears the Lord.
The Lord bless you from Zion:
    may you see the prosperity of Jerusalem
    all the days of your life.

℟. Blessed are those who fear the Lord.

Second Reading (I Thess 5:1-6)

Reflecting on Living the Gospel

When it comes to the "investments" of Christian living, the risks that make us "good and trustworthy" servants are found in the ordinary exchanges of daily life: forgiving rather than burying a grudge in our hearts; standing by another in times of sorrow, failure, or misunderstanding; associating with those some consider the "wrong kind" of people; laying down one's life for another—perhaps a misunderstood friend, a rebellious child, a terminally ill spouse, an aged parent. All this "now" effort is preparing us for the "not yet" entry into the kingdom.

Making Connections

The first reading echoes the idea that faithfulness in daily labors is how one lives out a lifelong commitment, whether that commitment is to one's spouse or to a life of faith. The second reading has those late fall pre-Advent vibes, when we are reminded of the end times and of our need to stay prepared. In light of the gospel and first reading, we know how to do this: through commitments to our small, daily acts of faith and love.

Psalmist Preparation

The idea of "walking" in God's ways is a lovely one for our life of ongoing growth in faith. It is a journey we make one step at a time, and the steps are often small ones. But our faithfulness is rewarded with fruitfulness—not always as visible as it is in this psalm's image of blissful domestic life, but real nonetheless. Think of one discipline in your own faith life that might be bettered by increased consistency; it might be a greater commitment to daily prayer or the regular practice of a work of mercy. Consider making a resolution and be sure to invite God into your intention. This can help make this psalm's response an earnest prayer: to persevere in faithfulness, we need God's blessing and accompaniment, each and every day.

Prayer

God of All Good Gifts,
Blessed are those who fear you,
and learn to walk in your ways.
Reward our labors, our service to your holy people,
and, at a time only you know,
bring all creation into oneness with each other and with you.
Amen.

Gospel (Matt 25:31-46; L160A)

Jesus said to his disciples: "When the Son of Man comes in his glory, and all the angels with him, he will sit upon his glorious throne, and all the nations will be assembled before him. And he will separate them one from another, as a shepherd separates the sheep from the goats. He will place the sheep on his right and the goats on his left. Then the king will say to those on his right, 'Come, you who are blessed by my Father. Inherit the kingdom prepared for you from the foundation of the world. For I was hungry and you gave me food, I was thirsty and you gave me drink, a stranger  and you welcomed me, naked and you clothed me, ill and you cared for me, in prison and you visited me.' Then the righteous will answer him and say, 'Lord, when did we see you hungry and feed you, or thirsty and give you drink? When did we see you a stranger and welcome you, or naked and clothe you? When did we see you ill or in prison, and visit you?' And the king will say to them in reply, 'Amen, I say to you, whatever you did for one of the least brothers of mine, you did for me.' Then he will say to those on his left, 'Depart from me, you accursed, into the eternal fire prepared for the devil and his angels. For I was hungry and you gave me no food, I was thirsty and you gave me no drink, a stranger and you gave me no welcome, naked and you gave me no clothing, ill and in prison, and you did not care for me.' Then they will answer and say, 'Lord, when did we see you hungry or thirsty or a stranger or naked or ill or in prison, and not minister to your needs?' He will answer them, 'Amen, I say to you, what you did not do for one of these least ones, you did not do for me.' And these will go off to eternal punishment, but the righteous to eternal life."

First Reading (Ezek 34:11-12, 15-17)

Thus says the Lord GOD:
> I myself will look after and tend my sheep.
As a shepherd tends his flock
> when he finds himself among his scattered sheep,
> so will I tend my sheep.

I will rescue them from every place where they were scattered
    when it was cloudy and dark.
I myself will pasture my sheep;
    I myself will give them rest, says the Lord God.
The lost I will seek out,
    the strayed I will bring back,
    the injured I will bind up,
    the sick I will heal,
    but the sleek and the strong I will destroy,
    shepherding them rightly.

As for you, my sheep, says the Lord God,
    I will judge between one sheep and another,
    between rams and goats.

Responsorial Psalm (Ps 23:1-2, 2-3, 5-6)

℞. (1) The Lord is my shepherd; there is nothing I shall want.

The Lord is my shepherd; I shall not want.
    In verdant pastures he gives me repose.

℞. The Lord is my shepherd; there is nothing I shall want.

Beside restful waters he leads me;
    he refreshes my soul.
He guides me in right paths
    for his name's sake.

℞. The Lord is my shepherd; there is nothing I shall want.

You spread the table before me
    in the sight of my foes;
you anoint my head with oil;
    my cup overflows.

℞. The Lord is my shepherd; there is nothing I shall want.

Only goodness and kindness follow me
    all the days of my life;
and I shall dwell in the house of the Lord
    for years to come.

℞. The Lord is my shepherd; there is nothing I shall want.

See Appendix, p. 218, for Second Reading

Reflecting on Living the Gospel

Those with power in our world are obligated to consider the welfare of all people—especially those who live on the margins of society. Christ showed a special concern for the overlooked and ostracized, even when doing so threatened social norms. Do we hold our leaders to these standards of compassion and inclusion? While we put our faith in Christ who is our ultimate leader and guide, we can also determine the legitimacy of our earthly leaders by noting how closely they follow the example of the Good Shepherd.

Making Connections

The first reading also has an image of leadership being turned upside down; shepherds were not people who commanded much respect in the ancient world, but it is them with whom God identifies. In the second reading, Paul affirms that Christ's power does not exist for its own sake. Rather, it is part of God's greater plan to restore us to right relationship with each other, with our world, and with God.

Psalmist Preparation

This psalm's familiarity can sometimes blunt its impact, especially for those of us who lead congregations in song and thus hear the songs so many times over as we rehearse and prepare. But this one is replete with beautiful imagery for God's leadership; it is not about control but about care. God grants those in his charge rest and nourishment, safety and satisfaction. As you prepare this psalm, spend a little time trying to rest in God's presence. Can you place yourself into God's care as you proclaim this psalm? It might invite others to do the same.

Prayer

God who Reigns,
your crown is of thorns, and your throne a rugged cross.
Your son's kingship is one of service and humility.
Indeed, *[t]he Lord is my shepherd,*
protecting and guiding,
anointing and preserving all life.
Help us all to love as Christ loves us,
finding him in the lowly and least in our midst.
Amen.

APPENDIX

FIRST SUNDAY OF ADVENT, November 27, 2022
Second Reading **(Rom 13:11-14)**

Brothers and sisters: You know the time; it is the hour now for you to awake from sleep. For our salvation is nearer now than when we first believed; the night is advanced, the day is at hand. Let us then throw off the works of darkness and put on the armor of light; let us conduct ourselves properly as in the day, not in orgies and drunkenness, not in promiscuity and lust, not in rivalry and jealousy. But put on the Lord Jesus Christ, and make no provision for the desires of the flesh.

SECOND SUNDAY OF ADVENT, December 4, 2022
Second Reading **(Rom 15:4-9)**

Brothers and sisters: Whatever was written previously was written for our instruction, that by endurance and by the encouragement of the Scriptures we might have hope. May the God of endurance and encouragement grant you to think in harmony with one another, in keeping with Christ Jesus, that with one accord you may with one voice glorify the God and Father of our Lord Jesus Christ.

Welcome one another, then, as Christ welcomed you, for the glory of God. For I say that Christ became a minister of the circumcised to show God's truthfulness, to confirm the promises to the patriarchs, but so that the Gentiles might glorify God for his mercy. As it is written:

> *Therefore, I will praise you among the Gentiles*
> *and sing praises to your name.*

THE IMMACULATE CONCEPTION OF THE BLESSED VIRGIN MARY, December 8, 2022
Second Reading **(Eph 1:3-6, 11-12)**

Brothers and sisters: Blessed be the God and Father of our Lord Jesus Christ, who has blessed us in Christ with every spiritual blessing in the heavens, as he chose us in him, before the foundation of the world, to be holy and without blemish before him. In love he destined us for adoption to himself through Jesus Christ, in accord with the favor of his will, for the praise of the glory of his grace that he granted us in the beloved.

In him we were also chosen, destined in accord with the purpose of the One who accomplishes all things according to the intention of his will, so that we might exist for the praise of his glory, we who first hoped in Christ.

THIRD SUNDAY OF ADVENT, December 11, 2022
Second Reading **(Jas 5:7-10)**

Be patient, brothers and sisters, until the coming of the Lord. See how the farmer waits for the precious fruit of the earth, being patient with it until it receives the early and the late rains. You too must be patient. Make your hearts firm, because the coming of the Lord is at hand. Do not complain, brothers and sisters, about one another, that you may not be judged. Behold, the Judge is standing before the gates. Take as an example of hardship and patience, brothers and sisters, the prophets who spoke in the name of the Lord.

FOURTH SUNDAY OF ADVENT, December 18, 2022
Second Reading (Rom 1:1-7)

Paul, a slave of Christ Jesus, called to be an apostle and set apart for the gospel of God, which he promised previously through his prophets in the holy Scriptures, the gospel about his Son, descended from David according to the flesh, but established as Son of God in power according to the Spirit of holiness through resurrection from the dead, Jesus Christ our Lord. Through him we have received the grace of apostleship, to bring about the obedience of faith, for the sake of his name, among all the Gentiles, among whom are you also, who are called to belong to Jesus Christ; to all the beloved of God in Rome, called to be holy. Grace to you and peace from God our Father and the Lord Jesus Christ.

THE NATIVITY OF THE LORD, *Vigil Mass*, December 25, 2022
Second Reading (Acts 13:16-17, 22-25)

When Paul reached Antioch in Pisidia and entered the synagogue, he stood up, motioned with his hand, and said, "Fellow Israelites and you others who are God-fearing, listen. The God of this people Israel chose our ancestors and exalted the people during their sojourn in the land of Egypt. With uplifted arm he led them out of it. Then he removed Saul and raised up David as king; of him he testified, 'I have found David, son of Jesse, a man after my own heart; he will carry out my every wish.' From this man's descendants God, according to his promise, has brought to Israel a savior, Jesus. John heralded his coming by proclaiming a baptism of repentance to all the people of Israel; and as John was completing his course, he would say, 'What do you suppose that I am? I am not he. Behold, one is coming after me; I am not worthy to unfasten the sandals of his feet.'"

THE NATIVITY OF THE LORD, *Mass at Midnight*, December 25, 2022
Second Reading (Titus 2:11-14)

Beloved: The grace of God has appeared, saving all and training us to reject godless ways and worldly desires and to live temperately, justly, and devoutly in this age, as we await the blessed hope, the appearance of the glory of our great God and savior Jesus Christ, who gave himself for us to deliver us from all lawlessness and to cleanse for himself a people as his own, eager to do what is good.

THE NATIVITY OF THE LORD, *Mass at Dawn*, December 25, 2022
Second Reading (Titus 3:4-7)

Beloved:
When the kindness and generous love
    of God our savior appeared,
not because of any righteous deeds we had done
    but because of his mercy,
he saved us through the bath of rebirth
    and renewal by the Holy Spirit,
whom he richly poured out on us
    through Jesus Christ our savior,
so that we might be justified by his grace
    and become heirs in hope of eternal life.

THE NATIVITY OF THE LORD, *Mass during the Day,*
December 25, 2022
Second Reading (Heb 1:1-6)

Brothers and sisters: In times past, God spoke in partial and various ways to our ancestors through the prophets; in these last days, he has spoken to us through the Son, whom he made heir of all things and through whom he created the universe,

who is the refulgence of his glory, the very imprint of his being,
and who sustains all things by his mighty word.
When he had accomplished purification from sins,
he took his seat at the right hand of the Majesty on high,
as far superior to the angels
as the name he has inherited is more excellent than theirs.

For to which of the angels did God ever say:

You are my son; this day I have begotten you?

Or again:

I will be a father to him, and he shall be a son to me?

And again, when he leads the firstborn into the world, he says:

Let all the angels of God worship him.

THE SOLEMNITY OF THE BLESSED VIRGIN MARY, MOTHER OF GOD,
January 1, 2023
Second Reading (Gal 4:4-7)

Brothers and sisters: When the fullness of time had come, God sent his Son, born of a woman, born under the law, to ransom those under the law, so that we might receive adoption as sons. As proof that you are sons, God sent the Spirit of his Son into our hearts, crying out, "Abba, Father!" So you are no longer a slave but a son, and if a son then also an heir, through God.

THE EPIPHANY OF THE LORD, January 8, 2023
Second Reading (Eph 3:2-3a, 5-6)

Brothers and sisters: You have heard of the stewardship of God's grace that was given to me for your benefit, namely, that the mystery was made known to me by revelation. It was not made known to people in other generations as it has now been revealed to his holy apostles and prophets by the Spirit: that the Gentiles are coheirs, members of the same body, and copartners in the promise in Christ Jesus through the gospel.

ASH WEDNESDAY, February 22, 2023
Second Reading (2 Cor 5:20–6:2)

Brothers and sisters: We are ambassadors for Christ, as if God were appealing through us. We implore you on behalf of Christ, be reconciled to God. For our sake he made him to be sin who did not know sin, so that we might become the righteousness of God in him.

Working together, then, we appeal to you not to receive the grace of God in vain. For he says:

In an acceptable time I heard you,
and on the day of salvation I helped you.

Behold, now is a very acceptable time; behold, now is the day of salvation.

FIRST SUNDAY OF LENT, February 26, 2023
Second Reading (Rom 5:12-19 [or Rom 5:12, 17-19])

Brothers and sisters: Through one man sin entered the world, and through sin, death, and thus death came to all men, inasmuch as all sinned— for up to the time of the law, sin was in the world, though sin is not accounted when there is no law. But death reigned from Adam to Moses, even over those who did not sin after the pattern of the trespass of Adam, who is the type of the one who was to come.

But the gift is not like the transgression. For if by the transgression of the one, the many died, how much more did the grace of God and the gracious gift of the one man Jesus Christ overflow for the many. And the gift is not like the result of the one who sinned. For after one sin there was the judgment that brought condemnation; but the gift, after many transgressions, brought acquittal. For if, by the transgression of the one, death came to reign through that one, how much more will those who receive the abundance of grace and of the gift of justification come to reign in life through the one Jesus Christ. In conclusion, just as through one transgression condemnation came upon all, so, through one righteous act, acquittal and life came to all. For just as through the disobedience of the one man the many were made sinners, so, through the obedience of the one, the many will be made righteous.

SECOND SUNDAY OF LENT, March 5, 2023
Second Reading (2 Tim 1:8b-10)

Beloved: Bear your share of hardship for the gospel with the strength that comes from God.

He saved us and called us to a holy life, not according to our works but according to his own design and the grace bestowed on us in Christ Jesus before time began, but now made manifest through the appearance of our savior Christ Jesus, who destroyed death and brought life and immortality to light through the gospel.

THIRD SUNDAY OF LENT, March 12, 2023
Second Reading (Rom 5:1-2, 5-8)

Brothers and sisters: Since we have been justified by faith, we have peace with God through our Lord Jesus Christ, through whom we have gained access by faith to this grace in which we stand, and we boast in hope of the glory of God.

And hope does not disappoint, because the love of God has been poured out into our hearts through the Holy Spirit who has been given to us. For Christ, while we were still helpless, died at the appointed time for the ungodly. Indeed, only with difficulty does one die for a just person, though perhaps for a good person one might even find courage to die. But God proves his love for us in that while we were still sinners Christ died for us.

FOURTH SUNDAY OF LENT, March 19, 2023
Second Reading (Eph 5:8-14)

Brothers and sisters: You were once darkness, but now you are light in the Lord. Live as children of light, for light produces every kind of goodness and righteousness and truth. Try to learn what is pleasing to the Lord. Take no part in the fruitless works of darkness; rather expose them, for it is shameful even to mention the things done by them in secret; but everything exposed by the light becomes visible, for everything that becomes visible is light. Therefore, it says: / "Awake, O sleeper, / and arise from the dead, / and Christ will give you light."

FIFTH SUNDAY OF LENT, March 26, 2023
Second Reading (Rom 8:8-11)
Brothers and sisters: Those who are in the flesh cannot please God. But you are not in the flesh; on the contrary, you are in the spirit, if only the Spirit of God dwells in you. Whoever does not have the Spirit of Christ does not belong to him. But if Christ is in you, although the body is dead because of sin, the spirit is alive because of righteousness. If the Spirit of the One who raised Jesus from the dead dwells in you, the One who raised Christ from the dead will give life to your mortal bodies also, through his Spirit dwelling in you.

PALM SUNDAY OF THE LORD'S PASSION, April 2, 2023
Second Reading (Phil 2:6-11)
Christ Jesus, though he was in the form of God,
    did not regard equality with God
    something to be grasped.
Rather, he emptied himself,
    taking the form of a slave,
    coming in human likeness;
    and found human in appearance,
    he humbled himself,
    becoming obedient to the point of death,
    even death on a cross.
Because of this, God greatly exalted him
    and bestowed on him the name
    which is above every name,
    that at the name of Jesus
    every knee should bend,
    of those in heaven and on earth and under the earth,
    and every tongue confess that
    Jesus Christ is Lord,
    to the glory of God the Father.

HOLY THURSDAY EVENING MASS OF THE LORD'S SUPPER, April 6, 2023
Second Reading (1 Cor 11:23-26)
Brothers and sisters: I received from the Lord what I also handed on to you, that the Lord Jesus, on the night he was handed over, took bread, and, after he had given thanks, broke it and said, "This is my body that is for you. Do this in remembrance of me." In the same way also the cup, after supper, saying, "This cup is the new covenant in my blood. Do this, as often as you drink it, in remembrance of me." For as often as you eat this bread and drink the cup, you proclaim the death of the Lord until he comes.

GOOD FRIDAY OF THE LORD'S PASSION, April 7, 2023
Second Reading (Heb 4:14-16; 5:7-9)

Brothers and sisters: Since we have a great high priest who has passed through the heavens, Jesus, the Son of God, let us hold fast to our confession. For we do not have a high priest who is unable to sympathize with our weaknesses, but one who has similarly been tested in every way, yet without sin. So let us confidently approach the throne of grace to receive mercy and to find grace for timely help.

In the days when Christ was in the flesh, he offered prayers and supplications with loud cries and tears to the one who was able to save him from death, and he was heard because of his reverence. Son though he was, he learned obedience from what he suffered; and when he was made perfect, he became the source of eternal salvation for all who obey him.

EASTER SUNDAY, April 9, 2023
Second Reading (1 Cor 5:6b-8 or [Col 3:1-4])

Brothers and sisters: Do you not know that a little yeast leavens all the dough? Clear out the old yeast, so that you may become a fresh batch of dough, inasmuch as you are unleavened. For our paschal lamb, Christ, has been sacrificed. Therefore, let us celebrate the feast, not with the old yeast, the yeast of malice and wickedness, but with the unleavened bread of sincerity and truth.

SECOND SUNDAY OF EASTER, April 16, 2023
Second Reading (1 Pet 1:3-9)

Blessed be the God and Father of our Lord Jesus Christ, who in his great mercy gave us a new birth to a living hope through the resurrection of Jesus Christ from the dead, to an inheritance that is imperishable, undefiled, and unfading, kept in heaven for you who by the power of God are safeguarded through faith, to a salvation that is ready to be revealed in the final time. In this you rejoice, although now for a little while you may have to suffer through various trials, so that the genuineness of your faith, more precious than gold that is perishable even though tested by fire, may prove to be for praise, glory, and honor at the revelation of Jesus Christ. Although you have not seen him you love him; even though you do not see him now yet believe in him, you rejoice with an indescribable and glorious joy, as you attain the goal of your faith, the salvation of your souls.

THIRD SUNDAY OF EASTER, April 23, 2023
Second Reading (1 Pet 1:17-21)

Beloved: If you invoke as Father him who judges impartially according to each one's works, conduct yourselves with reverence during the time of your sojourning, realizing that you were ransomed from your futile conduct, handed on by your ancestors, not with perishable things like silver or gold but with the precious blood of Christ as of a spotless unblemished lamb.

He was known before the foundation of the world but revealed in the final time for you, who through him believe in God who raised him from the dead and gave him glory, so that your faith and hope are in God.

FOURTH SUNDAY OF EASTER, April 30, 2023
Second Reading (1 Pet 2:20b-25)

Beloved: If you are patient when you suffer for doing what is good, this is a grace before God. For to this you have been called, because Christ also suffered for you, leaving you an example that you should follow in his footsteps.

He committed no sin, and no deceit was found in his mouth.

When he was insulted, he returned no insult; when he suffered, he did not threaten; instead, he handed himself over to the one who judges justly. He himself bore our sins in his body upon the cross, so that, free from sin, we might live for righteousness. By his wounds you have been healed. For you had gone astray like sheep, but you have now returned to the shepherd and guardian of your souls.

FIFTH SUNDAY OF EASTER, May 7, 2023
Second Reading (1 Pet 2:4-9)

Beloved: Come to him, a living stone, rejected by human beings but chosen and precious in the sight of God, and, like living stones, let yourselves be built into a spiritual house to be a holy priesthood to offer spiritual sacrifices acceptable to God through Jesus Christ. For it says in Scripture:

Behold, I am laying a stone in Zion,
a cornerstone, chosen and precious,
and whoever believes in it shall not be put to shame.

Therefore, its value is for you who have faith, but for those without faith:

The stone that the builders rejected
has become the cornerstone,

and

A stone that will make people stumble,
and a rock that will make them fall.

They stumble by disobeying the word, as is their destiny.

You are "a chosen race, a royal priesthood, a holy nation, a people of his own, so that you may announce the praises" of him who called you out of darkness into his wonderful light.

SIXTH SUNDAY OF EASTER, May 14, 2023
Second Reading (1 Pet 3:15-18)

Beloved: Sanctify Christ as Lord in your hearts. Always be ready to give an explanation to anyone who asks you for a reason for your hope, but do it with gentleness and reverence, keeping your conscience clear, so that, when you are maligned, those who defame your good conduct in Christ may themselves be put to shame. For it is better to suffer for doing good, if that be the will of God, than for doing evil. For Christ also suffered for sins once, the righteous for the sake of the unrighteous, that he might lead you to God. Put to death in the flesh, he was brought to life in the Spirit.

THE ASCENSION OF THE LORD, May 18 or 21, 2023
Second Reading (Eph 1:17-23)

Brothers and sisters: May the God of our Lord Jesus Christ, the Father of glory, give you a Spirit of wisdom and revelation resulting in knowledge of him. May the eyes of your hearts be enlightened, that you may know what is the hope that belongs to his call, what are the riches of glory in his inheritance among the holy ones, and what is the surpassing greatness of his power for us who believe, in accord with the exercise of his great might, which he worked in Christ, raising him from the dead and seating him at his right hand in the heavens, far above every principality, authority, power, and dominion, and every name that is named not only in this age but also in the one to come. And he put all things beneath his feet and gave him as head over all things to the church, which is his body, the fullness of the one who fills all things in every way.

SEVENTH SUNDAY OF EASTER, May 21, 2023
Second Reading (1 Pet 4:13-16)

Beloved: Rejoice to the extent that you share in the sufferings of Christ, so that when his glory is revealed you may also rejoice exultantly. If you are insulted for the name of Christ, blessed are you, for the Spirit of glory and of God rests upon you. But let no one among you be made to suffer as a murderer, a thief, an evildoer, or as an intriguer. But whoever is made to suffer as a Christian should not be ashamed but glorify God because of the name.

PENTECOST, May 28, 2023
Second Reading (1 Cor 12:3b-7, 12-13)

Brothers and sisters: No one can say, "Jesus is Lord," except by the Holy Spirit.

There are different kinds of spiritual gifts but the same Spirit; there are different forms of service but the same Lord; there are different workings but the same God who produces all of them in everyone. To each individual the manifestation of the Spirit is given for some benefit.

As a body is one though it has many parts, and all the parts of the body, though many, are one body, so also Christ. For in one Spirit we were all baptized into one body, whether Jews or Greeks, slaves or free persons, and we were all given to drink of one Spirit.

THE MOST HOLY TRINITY, June 4, 2023
Second Reading (2 Cor 13:11-13)

Brothers and sisters, rejoice. Mend your ways, encourage one another, agree with one another, live in peace, and the God of love and peace will be with you. Greet one another with a holy kiss. All the holy ones greet you.

The grace of the Lord Jesus Christ and the love of God and the fellowship of the Holy Spirit be with all of you.

THE MOST HOLY BODY AND BLOOD OF CHRIST, June 11, 2023
Second Reading (1 Cor 10:16-17)

Brothers and sisters: The cup of blessing that we bless, is it not a participation in the blood of Christ? The bread that we break, is it not a participation in the body of Christ? Because the loaf of bread is one, we, though many, are one body, for we all partake of the one loaf.

THE TRANSFIGURATION OF THE LORD, August 6, 2023
Second Reading (2 Pet 1:16-19)

Beloved: We did not follow cleverly devised myths when we made known to you the power and coming of our Lord Jesus Christ, but we had been eyewitnesses of his majesty. For he received honor and glory from God the Father when that unique declaration came to him from the majestic glory, "This is my Son, my beloved, with whom I am well pleased." We ourselves heard this voice come from heaven while we were with him on the holy mountain. Moreover, we possess the prophetic message that is altogether reliable. You will do well to be attentive to it, as to a lamp shining in a dark place, until day dawns and the morning star rises in your hearts.

THE ASSUMPTION OF THE BLESSED VIRGIN MARY, August 15, 2023
Second Reading (1 Cor 15:20-27)

Brothers and sisters: Christ has been raised from the dead, the firstfruits of those who have fallen asleep. For since death came through man, the resurrection of the dead came also through man. For just as in Adam all die, so too in Christ shall all be brought to life, but each one in proper order: Christ the firstfruits; then, at his coming, those who belong to Christ; then comes the end, when he hands over the Kingdom to his God and Father, when he has destroyed every sovereignty and every authority and power. For he must reign until he has put all his enemies under his feet. The last enemy to be destroyed is death, for "he subjected everything under his feet."

ALL SAINTS, November 1, 2023
Second Reading (1 John 3:1-3)

Beloved: See what love the Father has bestowed on us that we may be called the children of God. Yet so we are. The reason the world does not know us is that it did not know him. Beloved, we are God's children now; what we shall be has not yet been revealed. We do know that when it is revealed we shall be like him, for we shall see him as he is. Everyone who has this hope based on him makes himself pure, as he is pure.

THE SOLEMNITY OF OUR LORD JESUS CHRIST THE KING, November 26, 2023
Second Reading (1 Cor 15:20-26, 28)

Brothers and sisters: Christ has been raised from the dead, the firstfruits of those who have fallen asleep. For since death came through man, the resurrection of the dead came also through man. For just as in Adam all die, so too in Christ shall all be brought to life, but each one in proper order: Christ the firstfruits; then, at his coming, those who belong to Christ; then comes the end, when he hands over the kingdom to his God and Father, when he has destroyed every sovereignty and every authority and power. For he must reign until he has put all his enemies under his feet. The last enemy to be destroyed is death. When everything is subjected to him, then the Son himself will also be subjected to the one who subjected everything to him, so that God may be all in all.